Start with a Scan

SECOND EDITION

A Guide to Transforming
Scanned Images and Objects
into High-Quality Art

by

Janet Ashford and John Odam

PEACHPIT PRESS

Start with a Scan: A Guide to Transforming Scanned Images and Objects into High-Quality Art, Second Edition

Janet Ashford and John Odam

Peachpit Press
1249 Eighth Street
Berkeley, CA 94710
(800) 283-9444, (510) 524-2178
(510) 524-2221 (fax)

Find us on the World Wide Web at:
http://www.peachpit.com

Peachpit Press is a division of
Addison Wesley Longman.

Cover design: Janet Ashford and John Odam
Book design: Janet Ashford and John Odam
Production: Janet Ashford, John Odam, Doug
Isaacs and Lisa Brazieal

ISBN 0-201-71097-8

0 9 8 7 6 5 4 3 2

Printed and bound in the United States
of America.

DEDICATION

To my children—Rufus, Florence and Molly; and to my sweetheart, Tom.
—Janet Ashford

To Abby for her patience.
—John Odam

ACKNOWLEDGMENTS

We would like to thank the following people who served as photographic models: Rufus, Florence and Molly Ashford, Chris Caswell, Rachel Down, Doug Isaacs, Cynthia Llanos, Linda Margaretic, Janet Martini, George, Abby and Alison Odam, and Tony Yamane. All original photographs used in this book were taken by Janet Ashford and John Odam except as otherwise noted in the captions. (Some additional photographic elements were provided by Photodisc, Hulton/Deutsch and Image Club.) Thanks to Florence Ashford for permission to reproduce her photographic work.

Thanks to the Native American Renewable Energy Project, the Greyhound Adoption Center and Triad for permission to use graphics created for their Web pages and publications, and to Wadsworth and Greenhaven for permission to reproduce book covers and page designs.

Thanks also to Karin Arrigoni for her careful and rapid indexing and to Nancy Ruenzel and Victor Gavenda of Peachpit Press for their enthusiastic support of our project. And to Lisa Brazieal for her valiant efforts in production.

Many thanks to Doug Isaacs and Larry Christian of Adage Graphics in Los Angeles for their excellent service in producing film, and to Commercial Documentation Services in Oregon for direct-to-plate separations and printing.

Contents

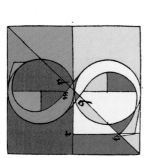

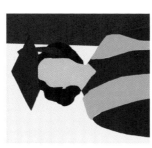

1 | Getting Started

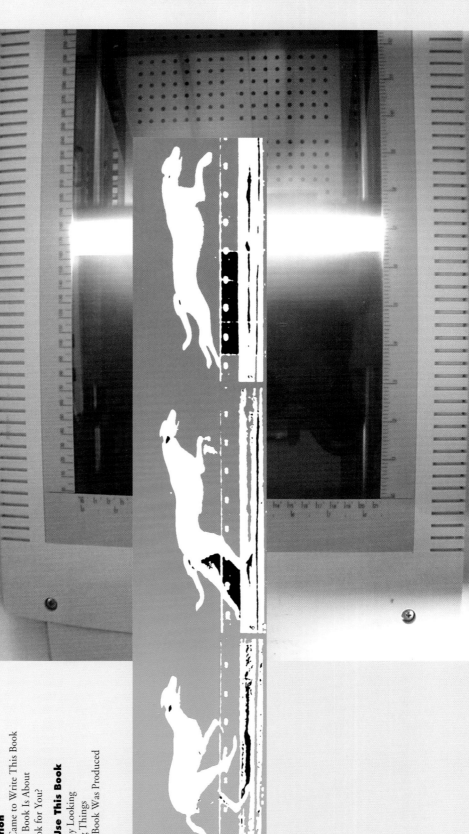

Introduction

HOW WE CAME TO WRITE THIS BOOK

Around 1989 I started writing books and "how-to" articles on computer graphics, describing in a step-by-step way how illustrators and graphic designers create their best work. After a while I noticed that almost every time I asked a computer artist how an image was created, the answer was "Well, I started with a scan of … " So, the idea was born for a book that would show how to transform raw scans into good-looking electronic illustrations. John and I published the first edition of *Start with a Scan* in 1996 and have since received many letters from readers who have found it helpful—not only as a guide to what can be done with scans, but as an inspiring source of graphic ideas.

For this second edition we've kept the book's original organization and text pretty much the same but we've created all new illustrations for every page and we've updated the instructions for the current versions of Photoshop and other programs. Also, we've added two new chapters—I've especially enjoyed creating Chapter 12, "Using Scans in Arts and Crafts" and John has contributed his expertise to Chapter 13, "Scanning for the Web."

I'm still convinced that a scanner is a *vital* tool for computer artists because it brings *non*-computer elements into the digital realm. Scanning provides the opportunity to incorporate the rich and irregular textures, colors and shapes of more traditional images—such as rough pencil sketches, pen-and-ink drawings, snapshots, old engravings, found art and so on—into our computer art so that it has more warmth, charm, humor and depth, as well as touches of appealing quirkiness. So once again, I hope you enjoy reading and using *Start with a Scan*.

—*Janet Ashford*

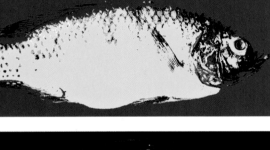

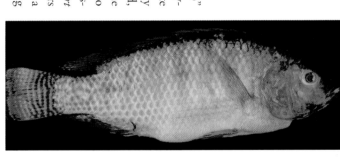

From ocean to desktop
This series of print effects produced by placing a fish on a scanner and manipulating color channels in Photoshop appeared in the first edition of *Start with a Scan.*

In the four years since the first edition of *Start with a Scan* was published there has been surge of inexpensive desktop scanners onto the market. What was once a specialty item found mainly in graphic design studios has become a widespread tool in homes, schools and businesses. In addition, after centuries of refinement, the commercial print media are having to share the stage as centers of progress in design. So in planning this new edition of *Start with a Scan* we wanted to include not only the mainstays of graphic design and desktop publishing—the process of communicating by multiple copies on printed paper—but also the one-of-a-kind, personal, and fine art uses of scanning, applied to a variety of media. This is a process that brings us full-circle back to the philosophy of the Craftsman era, but with the computer and scanner as our handy tools.

Another important development during this time has been the emergence of the Internet as a new visual medium. As with all new media, the Web is undergoing a rapid evolution that is raising technical and aesthetic questions about the appropriate use of scanning and digital imaging equipment. So in this edition we demonstrate some scanning and editing techniques that can speed the flow of visual information on-line.

Scanners today are much the same as they were four years ago, albeit cheaper. But image-editing software has gotten faster, more automated and more user-friendly. Many formerly complicated techniques that took a whole page to explain—such as drop shadows—can now be achieved with a couple of mouse clicks.

A lot has changed in the fast moving world of computer graphics, but what hasn't changed is the human eye and that which delights it.

—*John Odam*

From real to ideal
A "God's eye" made of yarn
and sticks was placed on a
scanner and scanned, then
sharpened in an image-editing
program to heighten its color
and contrast. A drop shadow
was added to make it appear to
rest on the page.

WHAT THIS BOOK IS ABOUT

Start with a Scan is a visual, step-by-step guide intended to show designers and illustrators how to transform raw scanned images into good-looking finished illustrations. The book includes three chapters (Chapters 2, 3 and 4) on the basics of scanning, to provide the technical information you need to get images out of the computer and onto the printed page. But the bulk of the book is devoted to showing you how to start with a scan of almost anything (a lackluster photo, a clip art engraving, a household object) and use either image-editing or PostScript illustration software to turn it into an original, high-quality piece of art.

In addition to our original chapters on using clip art, creating textures, working with photos, scanning real objects and so on, this second edition of *Start with a Scan* includes two new chapters. Chapter 12, "Using Scans in Arts and Crafts," shows how to take your scans out of the computer and into the crafter's world of paper, scissors and glue. Chapter 13, "Scanning for the Web," shows you how scanned photos and objects can be used in Web page design.

Every page in this second edition includes new illustrations in color and black-and-white, as well as clearly written text (updated for software changes), captions with how-to details, sidebars on special topics, and occasional quotes on related ideas, including creativity. We have again tried to make the book visually delightful, easy to browse through and read, well-organized, useful, and inspirational. With this book in hand you'll be able to:

• Learn how to start with a scan of *anything* and turn it into high-quality art.

• Browse through hundreds of full-color illustrations for ideas you can use.

• Follow clear, step-by-step instructions to get the results you want.

IS THIS BOOK FOR YOU?

Although *Start with a Scan* will be useful for anyone who owns a scanner (or digital camera) or is planning to get one, it is especially directed to those who use personal computers to create pages for publication, either on paper or on the Internet, professionally or just for fun.

We have two particular groups of readers in mind:

• first, experienced designers and illustrators who work with computer graphics every day and appreciate new ideas and techniques to stimulate their imaginations and broaden their repertoire,

• and second, design students and people who are new to the computer graphics field, who want to know what can be done in this medium.

If you have a love of visual images and a desire to tinker with them, this book's for you.

BACKGROUND AND SOFTWARE YOU WILL NEED

We assume that our professional readers are familiar with the most popular desktop graphics programs, including Adobe Photoshop, a PostScript drawing program (such as Macromedia FreeHand or Adobe Illustrator), an autotracing program (such as Adobe Streamline), and a page layout program (such as QuarkXPress or Adobe PageMaker or InDesign), on either a Macintosh or a Windows platform. With this background, you should be able to go directly from the book to your own computer to duplicate the effects you see on these pages. We don't include "click-and-drag" instructions for every technique because we want the book to be applicable for a variety of different software programs and computers. For the same reason, screen dumps and software menus are rarely included. But we do include enough detail so that you can translate from the system we're using to the one you're using. We do rely on Photoshop as our workhorse image-editor and we refer to Photoshop-specific features where necessary to clarify a procedure, knowing that other image-editing programs include similar functions.

How to Use This Book

LEARNING BY LOOKING

Start with a Scan is first and foremost a visual stimulus. Though we've made the text as clear and concise as possible, it should be possible to get a lot of information from this book simply by looking at the artwork, without reading a single word.

So first of all, look at it! *Start with a Scan* is packed with color illustrations designed to make you keep turning the pages, excite you about all the interesting things that can be done with a scan, and encourage you to try out our techniques yourself. The book is meant to stimulate your thinking about design and illustration, and about how you can expand the use of your scanner and computer as creative tools. As with some computer systems, the creative process sometimes "crashes." Keep this book handy when you're working out new ideas—it may keep you from getting stuck. When you see something you like and want to try, just read the caption next to the image. It will describe the technique in a quick, simple way that should get you started. For more details, and for background on the images and techniques, also read the running text.

ORGANIZING THINGS

We have divided the book into sections organized around the different ways scans can be used to generate original graphics for both print and the Web. If you are new to scanning you would be well-advised to begin with chapters 2, 3 and 4, which describe the basics of scanners, scanning and image-editing. Keep in mind though that this is not a book about scanning technique *per se*. Other books do an admirable job of explaining the technical aspects of scanning, including *Real World Scanning and Halftones, 2nd. Edition* by David Blatner, Glenn Fleishman and Steve Roth (Peachpit Press, 1998), which covers technical issues in depth. If you are already

familiar with the basics, we invite you to explore these pages in any order. For the most part, each page or spread is a self-contained explanation of a particular technique or resource.

Many of the original black-and-white scans from which images were made have been placed over a light green box so that they can be easily identified. We have also placed each piece of finished art (such as book covers, product labels, posters and so on) over a drop shadow that makes it easier to distinguish them from the step-by-step figures. Most sidebars are also placed over light green backgrounds and are self-contained small lessons on special topics.

HOW THIS BOOK WAS PRODUCED

The illustrations in this book were created using Adobe Photoshop and Image-Ready, Illustrator and PageMill, Macromedia FreeHand and Flash, Corel Painter and Altsys Fontographer. The book was designed and laid out in Adobe PageMaker. Photoshop was used for all image-editing. Janet used a Microtek ScanMaker X6EL scanner and John an Agfa Arcus II. We used Macintosh computers, but all the techniques shown here can be duplicated using the same programs running on Windows, and most can be used with other similar image-editing and drawing programs.

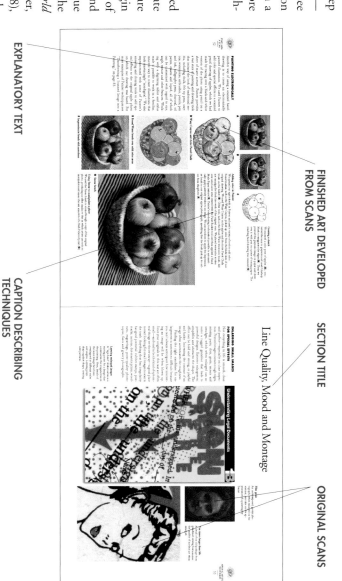

EXPLANATORY TEXT

FINISHED ART DEVELOPED FROM SCANS

CAPTION DESCRIBING TECHNIQUES

SECTION TITLE

Line Quality, Mood and Montage

ORIGINAL SCANS

2 | Working with Scanners

Scanners and Digitizing Devices
Types of Scanners
Digital Cameras, Digital Video Cameras

Scanners and Digitizing Devices

TYPES OF SCANNERS

Around 1985 we nearly bought a used stat camera. It was a deal. The main drawback was that a stat camera and its processing unit would take up a whole room. So we invested instead in a Macintosh computer, without realizing that soon this curious hybrid of a TV set and a typewriter would be hooked up to a scanning device far more powerful and versatile than a room-filling stat camera (and a lot cheaper, too). Today, the ubiquitous scanner has not only replaced the old stat camera, but has also made remarkable inroads into the color separation industry. Prices have tumbled, too. A perfectly capable color scanner can be purchased nowadays for less than $100. Here are some of the main types.

DRUM

The drum scanner is the typical "high-end" equipment used by color separators who make the film used for printing. It uses a *photomultiplier tube* (PMT) as a sensor to capture the image. PMTs accurately measure the light and dark value of an image line-by-line vertically as the drum rapidly revolves. Filters are used to extract the color information. Drum scanners can cost as much as $50,000. Most use specialized software and hardware and are geared toward the maximum quality of resolution and color fidelity. Recently, lower-cost, scaled-down versions of drum scanners have been introduced for the desktop market.

FLATBED

The typical workhorse scanner used in desktop publishing is the flatbed. Ranging in price from $100 to $2,000, most operate at 1-bit (line art), 8-bit grayscale (256 grays), and 24-bit/36 bit color (over 16 million colors). Flatbed scanners use an array of *charge-coupled devices*

(CCDs) to convert the image to digital information, reading the image in a series of horizontal strips.

Two basic flatbed scanner types are currently available: three-pass and one-pass. A *three-pass scanner* uses one light source and three filters to generate the RGB (red, green, blue) values needed for a color scan; the light source travels across the original three times. *One-pass scanners* use either three separate strobe lights (red, green and blue), that flash alternately in rapid succession as the scanning mechanism passes once across the original, or a prism to split the beam from a single white light source via filters into rays of red, green and blue light. Although some three-pass scanners may produce more accurate

Charge-Coupled Device (CCD)

images they are slower than one-pass scanners.

FLATBED/SLIDE

Some flatbed scanners are also equipped with another light source in the lid that allow slides, negatives and transparencies to be scanned. Transparency scanning is more exacting since the originals are smaller. It's worth noting that unless a flatbed/slide scanner has an *optical resolution* of 2000 pixels per inch or more, it will not do justice to 35mm slides and negatives. (For more on optical resolution see page 10).

SLIDE SCANNER

Dedicated slide scanners are available in the $500 to $3,000 price range and are mostly limited to the 35 mm format. They are particularly useful to commercial photographers who like to provide their clients with digital images, or who use their slides to create photo montages on the computer. Some slide scanners are designed for internal installation in the computer. Although the image quality from a slide scanner is good, its quality is not quite as high as a drum scanner.

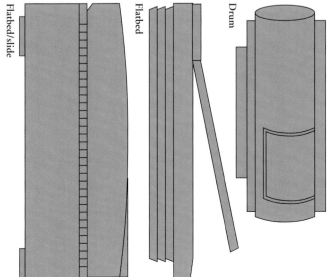

Drum

Flatbed

Flatbed/slide

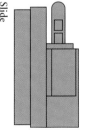

Slide

The four basic kinds of scanners used in graphic arts Since their introduction in 1987, the number of desktop scanners in use has grown to over 20 million throughout the world.

An economical alternative to owning a slide scanner is to have your slides or color negatives digitized onto a Kodak Photo CD disk at cost of $1 to $3 per image. For quality rivaling the drum scanner it might be worth waiting over a week for the processing.

OTHER SCANNER TYPES

The once-popular hand-held scanner has fallen out of favor and is no longer marketed. Another oddity is the combination scanner/fax printer, an all purpose tool that sacrifices some quality for the sake of convenience.

DIGITAL CAMERAS, DIGITAL VIDEO CAMERAS

Other ways of capturing visual information digitally do not involve scanning.

DIGITAL CAMERAS

Digital cameras also use CCD sensors. Since a digital camera must capture the image in a fraction of a second it uses a matrix of millions of sensors, one for each pixel in the image. As might be expected, few digital cameras have the resolution capability of a typical camera, but all of them can produce images suitable for on-screen display and Web pages, and many can produce 8 by 10-inch prints of very high quality.

DIGITAL VIDEO CAMERAS

Another useful source of images is digital video cameras which, unlike their analog counterparts, can produce sharp stills at 640 × 480 pixels.

If you have either a digital camera or a digital video camera but do not own a scanner, you will find that most of this book will be useful since all of the many ways of using and transforming a scan can be applied to any digitized image.

HOW A CHARGE-COUPLED DEVICE WORKS

A charge-coupled device (CCD) is an array of tiny elements—up to 3,000 mounted on a chip in three rows (**A**). The function of the CCD is to measure the intensity of light reflected from thousands of small areas of the original and convert these measurements to digital information. In a three-pass scanner, the CCD has a single array of elements, as shown in the diagram. A one-pass scanner has three arrays coated with red, green and blue.

In this detail of the CCD array (**B**), the central row of silicon elements is light-sensitive. Light striking an element generates a negative charge proportional to the amount of light it receives. The two outside rows of elements carry the charge away from the central elements at regular intervals, resetting the light-sensitive elements to neutral. These elements read out the charge as digital pulses that are transmitted to the surrounding circuitry. This light-sampling process is rather like having a row of buckets in a field during a rainstorm, where the water level in the buckets is measured at regular intervals and the buckets are emptied to begin again.

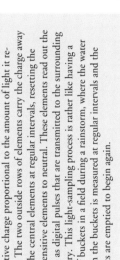

A

CCD unit
mounted on
circuit board

Negative charge

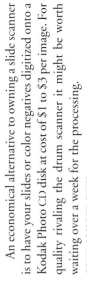

Light

Receptor element

Readout element

B

HOW A SCANNER WORKS

When you click the mouse to start scanning, here's what happens:

(**A**) Commands from the computer instruct the logic board (**1**) to regulate the motor speed controller (**2**) and motor (**3**). The motor drives the transmission belt (**4**), which is connected to the scanning unit (**5**).

These logic board instructions move the scanning unit into the correct position to begin the scan; they also govern the speed of the motor during the scan. Light from the lamps (**6**) strikes the original artwork or photograph placed facedown on the glass top and is reflected from the mirrors (**7**) through the lens (**8**) and onto the CCD sensors (**9**).

Output from the CCD sensors is interpreted by the logic board and transmitted back to the computer.

(**B**) A section through the scanning unit that travels under the glass top shows two mirrors angled so that the light reflected from the original passes through a lens and is focused on the CCD sensors.

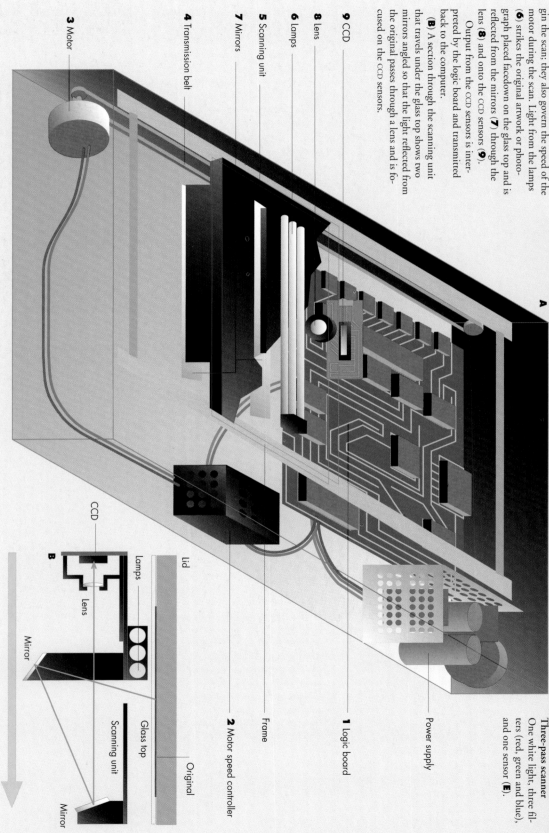

3 Motor

4 Transmission belt

7 Mirrors

5 Scanning unit

6 Lamps

8 Lens

9 CCD

1 Logic board

2 Motor speed controller

Frame

Power supply

B

CCD

Lens

Mirror

Lamps

Lid

Glass top

Scanning unit

Original

Mirror

Three-pass scanner
One white light, three filters (red, green and blue), and one sensor (**E**).

Red, green, blue filters

CCD

E

Two types of one-pass scanners
Three lights (red, green and blue) beamed at one sensor (**C**). One white light, a beam-splitting prism, and three sensors (red, green and blue) (**D**).

C
CCD

D
Red, green, blue CCDs

Beam splitter

A

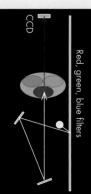

3 | Technical Considerations

Planning Ahead

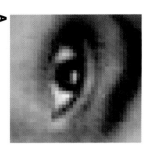

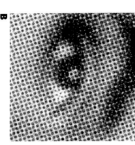

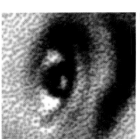

HOW WILL YOUR SCAN BE USED?

Scanning is the first step in a series that leads to producing an image in some type of media. Knowing how your scan will be used is essential in determining your first step. Will your scan be used in high-quality offset color printing in sizes larger than 8 by 10 inches? If so, you may require scans from commercial color separators. Most desktop scanning equipment can't record the amount of information needed for full-page advertisements, large-format books, calendars, posters, and so on. However, a desktop scanner *can* produce excellent results for offset printing in all but the most exacting cases. For example, if the original is a regular (continuous-tone) print, in color or black-and-white, 8 by 10 inches or less, and your output size is 100% or less of the original size, you can make good-quality images suitable for offset printing. Desktop scanners are perfect of course for preliminary design work and output to any kind of inkjet or laser printer, all of which have less stringent resolution requirements. Desktop scanners are also excellent for capturing images for on-screen multimedia presentations and Web pages, for which the resolution need not be higher than 72 dpi.

FROM SCANNER TO PRINT

OFFSET PRINTING

Pixels—short for *picture elements*—are the "atoms" that comprise computer images. A grid of tiny pixels forms a mosaic of adjacent squares of different colors or gray tones which, when viewed from a distance, makes up a smooth looking image. The resolution or fineness of a scanned image is determined by the number of *pixels per inch* (ppi). (Resolution is also sometimes referred to as *dots per inch* or dpi.)

By contrast, a printed image is usually created by a halftone screen composed of a mesh of tiny dots that

OPTICAL RESOLUTION

The *optical resolution* of a scanner is determined by the density of its array of CCDs. You can check the optical resolution of your scanner by reading the manual or contacting the manufacturer. Optical resolution fixes an absolute limit on the amount of information the scanner can extract from an original.

INTERPOLATION

Most scanning software allows scanning at several times the built-in optical resolution of the scanner. This is

vary in size (darker areas are produced by larger dots). Superimposed halftone screens in four colors—cyan, magenta, yellow and black—make up a printed color image. The fineness of a halftone screen is determined by the number of *lines* or rows of dots *per inch* (lpi).

The matrix of pixels that makes up a scanned image is displayed on the monitor and stored in the computer's memory. But to create a printed image that information has to be interpreted by a *raster image processor* (RIP) in an output device and converted to halftone dots which are printed on paper or on the film used for making printing plates. When scanned images are output as halftone dots through an imagesetter, the halftone dots themselves are made up of tiny imagesetter dots.

DESKTOP PRINTING

Toner-based laser printers, both color and black-and-white, use a coarser version of the same halftone screen technique used in offset printing. Inkjet printers, on the other hand, use a random pattern of fine ink dots, known as a *stochastic* printing. It is the distance between the dots, and not their size, that determines the tone and color. Stochastic printing has the advantage of producing very high definition prints from relatively low-resolution images.

Composing an image

In a digital scan the image is made of a grid of pixels of varying shades of color (**A**), whereas in a printer's halftone (**B**) the picture is composed of round dots that vary in size. In an inkjet print ink dots of identical size are clustered in a random pattern with varying density (**C**).

C

Interpolation

Compared with a scan made at the scanner's optical resolution (shown in detail) (**D**), a scan made at twice that resolution adds more pixels but not more information (**E**). Interpolation fills in the missing information by averaging the differences between neighboring pixels.

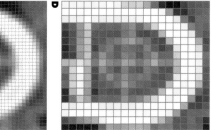

E

D

achieved by *interpolation*, a process that spreads out the information collected by the CCDs over a larger area and fills in the missing pixels by averaging. Interpolation adds resolution—but not detail—to an image.

GETTING THE MOST OUT OF YOUR SCANNER

All scanning processes require software to integrate the scanning hardware with the rest of your computer system. There are basically three software options: using the software that comes with the scanner, using a "plug-in" module that links your scanner to an image-editing program, or using third-party software that is designed to work with many different scanners and includes color-correction, automatic exposure and other controls. No matter which option you use, you will be able to specify resolution via the software before the scan is made. Typical settings range from 50 to 2,400 ppi or dpi. Some scanning software includes features that help you choose the appropriate resolution for a scan, depending on its purpose.

Scanning at the highest possible resolution is not a good idea since it consumes time and disk space and produces more digital information than you need. The ideal to aim for is an "optimal resolution" in which the scan resolution provides just as much information as the output and printing processes can effectively use, and no more.

OPTIMAL RESOLUTION FOR HALFTONE OUTPUT

The three main factors that affect the quality of a printed halftone image are:

The number of pixels per inch in the scan (ppi)

The number of lines per inch in the halftone (lpi)

The scale of the final image (%)

The process of converting square pixels into round printers' dots requires that there be roughly two pixels

SCANNING SLIDES

Transparencies have a density range up to 10 times that of prints, which gives them a crisp quality and explains why slides are preferred by professional photographers and color separators. But transparencies are challenging to scan. For one thing, blemishes that go unnoticed on prints are glaringly evident on slides. One should avoid touching the surface of slides to avoid leaving finger marks. Dust can be removed by using a soft brush or a compressed air canister.

In this side-by-side comparison, we scanned a 35mm slide on

an Agfa Arcus II at 1200 ppi—the maximum optical resolution of this model (**A**). The lettering on the crate looks a little fuzzy, while it's clearly legible on the original through a loupe. The same slide was sent out for processing on a Kodak Photo CD. There is a noticeable gain in image quality, apparent in the blowup insert (**B**).

As might be expected, larger format transparencies such as 2¼-inch square and 4 by 5 inches produce better quality scans than postage stamp-sized 35mm slides.

of image information for every printed halftone dot, so it's usually recommended that the pixels per inch (ppi) of the scan be twice the lines per inch of the halftone (lpi). We have found, however, that a ratio of 1.67 ppi/lpi provides optimal resolution. So, for example, if your image will be printed with a 133 lpi screen, it should be scanned at 222 ppi (133 × 1.67). We practice what we preach: all the images in this book were

scanned at 250 ppi and printed at 150 lpi; a ratio of exactly 1.67 ppi/lpi, except for fine line engravings (such as those in Chapter 5) which retain more detail when scanned at 300 dpi.

SCALE AND RESOLUTION

Scanning at 100 ppi at 200% produces the same number of pixels as scanning at 200 ppi at 100%. The

Scaling a scanned image
Left to right: 72 ppi at 100%; 72 ppi at 33%, equivalent to 216 ppi; 72 ppi at 300%, equivalent to 24 ppi.

difference will be the dimensions and ppi of the image when it's imported into a layout, drawing or image-editing program. Scaling an image up or down after it has been placed in a layout program also affects its resolution. A 72 ppi image scaled down to 33% in a layout program has an effective resolution of 216 ppi, but if it's scaled up 300%, its resolution will be only 24 ppi.

Here's a formula for calculating the optimal resolution for a scan (in pixels per inch) that also takes scaling into account:

$$\frac{\text{Final image width}}{\text{Original image width}} \times \text{lpi} \times 1.67$$

RESOLUTION FOR DESKTOP PRINTING
Inkjet and laser printers have much lower resolution requirements than those of offset printing. In most cases 150 ppi is sufficient and some manufacturers recommend only 100 ppi. An optimal resolution formula for desktop output is:

$$\frac{\text{Final image width}}{\text{Original image width}} \times 150$$

RESOLUTION FACTORS IN LINE ART
Since line art files are small compared with grayscale or color files, there is no reason to forgo your scanner's maximum optical resolution to get the best-quality output. There's little to be gained, however, by exceeding 1200 pixels per inch.

SCAN RESOLUTION (ppi)

50   100   150   225   250   300

HALFTONE SCREEN FREQUENCY (lpi)

Resolution and quality in offset printing
To demonstrate how the relationship between halftone screen frequency (lpi) and scanning resolution (ppi or dpi) effects printed quality, we show the same image at six different resolutions from left to right—50, 100, 150, 225, 250 and 300 ppi, and at three different halftone screen frequencies from bottom to top—50, 100 and 150 lpi. For this book, which is printed with a line screen of 150 lpi, we chose to scan our continuous tone images at 250 ppi.

Preparation, Formats and Modes

GETTING READY FOR SCANNING

Clean glass surfaces are important to ensure an immaculate image. We always wipe them down with glass cleaner before scanning. Any blemish—such as dust or scratches on the slide, the photo print or on the scanner glass—will be visible in the scan. We recommend blowing off the dust with a blow brush or compressed air canister. Using a mount to keep transparencies out of contact with the glass helps keep them in focus and avoids interference patterns. You may also want to calibrate your monitor so that you can be more accurate in assessing color balance as you scan.

PREPARING THE ORIGINAL

Many desktop scanners are capable of scanning several different types of originals. Originals may include prints (reflective images), or film (slides, negatives and transparencies). An ideal print is a continuous-tone color or black and white photograph, no bigger than 8.5×11 inches, on opaque paper. Originals that are already halftones pose special problems: moiré patterns and possible copyright violations (see pages 24 and 28). If the original is on thin paper with something printed on the back, there may be show-through that will be picked up by the scanner. The easy solution is to place a sheet of black paper behind the original and adjust the brightness if necessary. An ideal transparency original is a large-format film at 4×5-inch or $2\frac{1}{4} \times 2\frac{1}{4}$-inch size.

POSITIONING THE ORIGINAL

For best results, place the original in the dead center of the scanning area. Originals placed at the edge are using only the periphery of the scanning lens and will not be as sharply focused.

Some scanning software automatically compensates for crooked originals. It can save time, however, if your original is already straight. Butting the edge of the original to the edge of the glass will ensure a straight scan. Close the lid *slowly* so that escaping air doesn't blow your original off kilter. If the original is out of square—for example, a smaller image taped casually to a larger piece of paper—use a T-square, cutting board and X-Acto knife to trim the edge of the larger paper in alignment with the taped image.

When your original is not straight on its page, you may have to use the preview mode of your scanning software to check alignment. Straightening a scan in preview mode is counter-intuitive: move the original in the *same* direction that it appears to be leaning.

BIT DEPTH AND SCANNING MODES

Bit depth refers to the amount of digital information embedded in each pixel. Most scanning software provides for these bit-depth options:

1-bit	Black and white
8-bit	256 shades of gray
24-bit	16.7 million colors

Other options might include 36-bit color, 16-bit grayscale, 8-bit color, 256 colors, and "halftone." The halftone mode is intended for the older dot-matrix or similar printers that cannot generate their own halftones to reproduce grayscale images.

We've found that the most useful scanning modes are 16.7 million colors and 256 shades of gray. For various reasons, these are the only ones that can be successfully edited in Photoshop. Options for editing 1-bit black-and-white images are limited so it's wise to scan line art in grayscale mode first and convert it to 1-bit mode after editing. The "256 shades of gray" scanning mode is best for use with monochrome originals such as black-and-white photos.

SCANNING IN GRAYSCALE OR CONVERTING FROM COLOR: DOES IT MAKE A DIFFERENCE?

When you need a black-and-white scan of a color original you can either scan it in grayscale or scan it in color and convert it to grayscale later in an image-editing program.

The first method is quicker, but uses only the green channel to record the image. A full-color scan gives more balanced tonal information which is preserved when the RGB file is converted to grayscale in an image-editing program such as Photoshop.

Color scan

Color scan converted to grayscale in Photoshop

Grayscale scan

FILE FORMATS

Which file format is the best for saving finished scans? The answer will depend on how the scan is going to be used and what operating system you are using, but the general strategy is to save in the most universal format for all possible applications and platforms.

TIFFS

TIFF, the acronym for *tagged image file format*, is the most widely used image format in print media. TIFF files can be read by all image-editing programs and they can be placed in all layout programs. In addition, many PostScript illustration programs can import TIFF files either as templates for tracing or for incorporation into the artwork. A TIFF file can be in color, grayscale or line art mode. Color images are scanned in RGB mode by the scanner, but can be converted to CMYK mode if that is required. Grayscale images can be converted to line art by dithering, an effect akin to a mezzotint.

PICTS, GIFS AND JPEG

PICT files are used in multimedia and animation. On-line images for the Internet should be saved as GIF files, or as compressed JPEG files. (For more about file formats for the Web, see page 128 "Using Scans On-line".)

HANDLING LARGE ORIGINALS

Don't worry if your original is larger than the scanning window. The limiting factors for image size are computer memory and human patience, not the size of your scanner. Tiling the scan and welding the pieces together in your image-processing software is relatively easy, provided that you allow some overlap and that initial scans are straight. A digital camera will take in the entire image in one step, but its resolution limitations will restrict the size of the reproduction.

Scanning oversize art
This original watercolor, made by John Odam in a life-drawing class, measures 12 by 16 inches. However, the maximum image area of his flatbed scanner is 8.5 by 11.7 inches. The scanning was done in two overlapping sections (**A**). John lined up the edge of the watercolor paper with the edge of the scanning area to get the image straight. In Photoshop he extended the vertical canvas size of the top half of the image and pasted the bottom half carefully into position forming a second layer. He zoomed in to check alignment and used the nudge keys for final positioning (**B**). To disguise the seam he selected the overlap on the top layer, feathered the selection and deleted it (**C**).

A

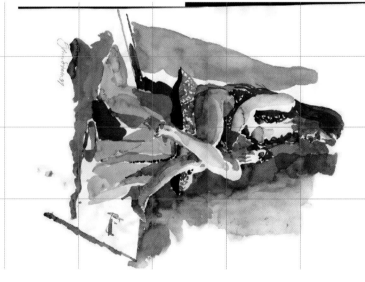

B

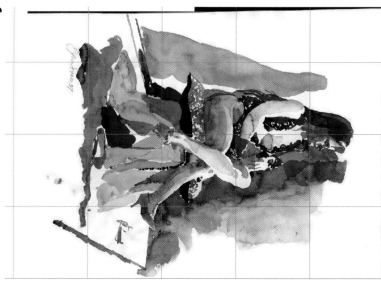

C

4 Editing Scanned Images

Working with Tone and Color

IMPROVING IMAGE QUALITY

Once you've made a scan at the appropriate resolution for your intended use, it's time to open use an image-editing program to check the quality of the image. Does it have good contrast? Is the color balance accurate and pleasing? Is the picture well-focused? Are there dust specks or scratches? Plan the sequencing of any fix-up work. In general, it's best to correct tonal range and color balance first, for if these cannot be improved, the image may have to be discarded. Next make any necessary changes in the content of the image—for example repairing torn areas, cropping to improve the composition, and so on—and then sharpen the image. Most photographs, no matter how poorly exposed, out of focus, or badly composed, can be significantly improved with electronic darkroom tools! We use Photoshop for image-editing and that program's specific functions and tools are referred to in this chapter. Similar tools are available in other image-editing programs, including Painter, PhotoDeluxe, PaintShop Pro and Photo-Paint.

CALIBRATION

Before you attempt any corrections to tonal range and color balance, it's important that your system be calibrated so that there is a predictable relationship between what you see on-screen and what you get when your art is output to paper or film. Your "system" includes your monitor, scanner, scanning and image-editing software, and output device (printer or imagesetter). Refer to the materials that came with your system components for information on calibration.

IMPROVING TONAL RANGE

Tonal range refers to the range of light and dark areas in an image and is a concern for both black-and-white and color scans. Unless the subject is something like a ski slope or a cave, an image should have a full range of midtone values between white and black. But note that many prepress professionals suggest that the end points of the tonal scale should not be 100 percent black or 100 percent white but should be set at percentages of, for example, 3% black for white and 97% black for black images, adjustments to tonal range are usually made to the full RGB image, but they can also be made to each color channel individually if you are trying to remove a color cast, for example.

BRIGHTNESS AND CONTRAST

When faced with a muddy picture, it seems easiest to use the Brightness and Contrast controls. But these only shift the entire image up or down in brightness, without changing the relationship between the two extremes and the midtones. So in trying to lighten or darken the midtones you may blow out the highlights (make them too white) or plug up the shadows with black. You'll have more control by using histogram controls (Levels in Photoshop) or a Gamma curve (Curves in Photoshop).

WHAT IS A HISTOGRAM?

A "histogram" is a graph display that plots the dark to light values of a continuous-tone image along the x, or horizontal, axis and the number of pixels found at each lightness value on the y, or vertical, axis. Whenever an image is open in Photoshop, the Levels command provides a dialog box with a histogram (labeled "Input") which displays the current tonal range of the image. The Levels command can be used to adjust contrast by resetting the black and white points and also to edit the midtones independently of the shadows and highlights.

(see "Dot Gain: The Screen Lies" on page 17). In color

A Original image with corresponding Levels histogram

SETTING THE BLACK AND WHITE POINTS

Defining values for the darkest and lightest pixels in an image is the first tonal range adjustment to make. This is called "setting black and white points." In a given image, "black" and "white" might have values of 10 and 240 respectively, over a total of 256 possible levels of gray (or brightness) from 0 to 255. Resetting the black and white points to 0 and 255 will usually improve contrast by spreading the brightness values of the pixels over a broader range and can be done automatically by clicking the Auto button in the Levels dialog box. Photoshop 5.5 and later versions also include a new Auto Contrast command which improves contrast while preventing shifts in color.

If you're not happy with the results of automatic controls, you can adjust the black and white points manually. For example, pulling the black and white sliders inward on the Levels Input scale (thus shortening the range of the input image) remaps those values out to 0 and 255 on the output scale, which increases contrast.

B Increasing contrast through Photoshop's Brightness/Contrast controls

C Increasing contrast by clicking Auto in the Levels dialog to reset black and white points.

D Increasing contrast by choosing Auto Contrast.

E Increasing contrast by moving Input black and white sliders inward

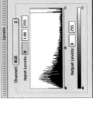

Histogram after using Brightness/contrast controls

Histogram after using Auto button to reset black and white points

Histogram after choosing the Auto Contrast command

Histogram after using black and white Input sliders to reset black and white points

Improving contrast

A photo of a bridge over the Arno in Florence was taken on a cloudy day and lacked contrast. The histogram for the image, displayed in the Levels dialog box in Photoshop, shows a lack of pixels at the extreme ends of black and white, a concentration of pixels at the dark end of the range and a spike at the light end (**A**). An easy way to increase contrast in an image like this is to increase the contrast in the Contrast/Brightness dialog box. But doing so produces an image in which the sky is too white (**B**). A more effective way to improve contrast is to increase the width of the tonal range of the image by resetting the black and white points to 0 and 255. This spreads all the tonal values over the full range of 256 possible gray or brightness levels. Resetting the black and white points can be done automatically by clicking on the Auto button in Photoshop's Levels dialog box. Our resetting produced an increase in contrast in the midtones without dramatically increasing the brightness of the highlights or the darkness of the shadows. However the sky suffers from a slight bluish color cast (**C**). Another way to improve contrast is to use Photoshop's new Auto Contrast command, which does a similar job of resetting the black and white points, while avoiding the color cast (**D**). The black and white points can also be set "manually" by moving the black and white sliders on the Input scale in the Levels dialog box inward toward the center, which reduces the tonal range of the original image and remaps it outward to the full output range of 256 gray levels, thus in effect resetting the black and white points at the values you choose. In the bridge image, we moved the black and white sliders inward to positions just inside the edges of the spread of pixels (**E**). This produced an image with improved contrast and good detail in the midtones, very similar to the result produced by the Auto Contrast Command.

DOT GAIN: THE SCREEN LIES

Dot gain is what happens when the ink in a halftone dot spreads out when it's printed on paper. The ink will spread only slightly on coated paper, more on uncoated paper and even more on newsprint. Unfortunately, this means that even though your image may look terrific on the screen, when printed on paper it may be too dark, with muddy midtones and lost detail in shadow areas.

To overcome dot gain problems we recommend first editing the file to optimize the way the image looks on screen. Once you're satisfied, save it and then create a duplicate file to correct before sending out for film. If you are working in Photoshop, the adjustments should be made in the Input/Output Levels controls in the Levels dialog box. Ask your printer how much dot gain correction you should use and whether to adjust for dot gain in the midtones or in the shadows—or both.

To make dot gain corrections in the midtones, change the number in the middle box next to the words "Input levels," which is set to a default of 1.00. Entering 1.35 would make a 10% reduction and entering 1.95 would make a 20% reduction in dot size, for example (because the entire tonal range is contains 256 levels). For corrections to shadows, enter a value in the first box to the right of the words "Output Levels." A value of 30, for example, would cause a 10% reduction and a value of 55 would make a 20% reduction.

Then check the results. The screen may lie, but the Info Palette always tells the truth about dot percentages. Use it by placing your cursor over the highlight, midtone and shadow areas of your image to show the dot percentage you will get on film. When adjusting Input/Output levels, the Info palette displays what the inking values will be before and after the corrections are applied.

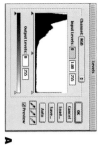

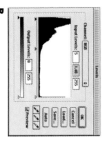

Editing midrange values with Levels controls

This photo of freshly picked zucchini squash is dark and lacks contrast in the midrange blues and greens. A histogram of the image shows how the pixels are skewed to the dark end of the input brightness scale (**A**). Moving the gray slider to the left lightens the midtones (**B**). The histogram for the edited image shows how the distribution of pixels has spread over more of the tonal range (**C**), greatly improving detail in the midtones of the image.

EDITING MIDRANGE VALUES

The Levels histogram also includes a gray slider on the Input scale that makes it possible to edit the midtones. To brighten, move the gray slider to the left; to darken them, move it to the right. By moving the gray slider you are actually changing the *gamma* of the image. Adjusting the gamma curve makes it possible to change contrast and brightness in the middle range of tones without noticeably effecting the deep shadows and bright highlights.

WHAT IS GAMMA?

"Gamma" or "gamma curve" refers to a line or curve that describes the relationship between the input and output brightness of an image; or, more simply, between the brightness values in an original, unedited scan and those in the scan after it's been edited. In Photoshop the gamma curve is displayed in the Curves dialog box. The brightness values of the "input" (the scanned original) are shown along the *x*, or horizontal, axis and the brightness values of the "output" (an edited version of the original) are shown along the *y*, or vertical, axis. In an unedited scan, the gamma is initially set at a value of 1 (all the input values are equal to the output values) and the gamma "curve" is actually a straight diagonal line at 45 degrees. When changes are made to this gamma curve, the tonal values of the image change.

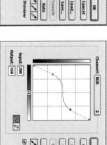

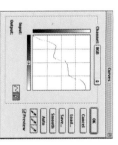

Changing a gamma curve

In Photoshop a gamma curve (**D**) can be redrawn either by placing points along the curve and bending it by dragging a points (**E**), or by drawing a new curve using the pencil tool provided in the Curves dialog box (**F**).

CHANGING GAMMA

WITH SCANNER SOFTWARE

Some scanners make it possible to set gamma and black and white points within the scanning software before the scan is made. (To capture the widest dynamic range possible, the Photoshop manual recommends that black and white points be set by the scanner.) Look at the manual that came with your scanner software to learn what adjustments can be made during the scanning process. In general a gamma setting below 1 darkens the midtones while a gamma above 1 lightens the midtones.

WITH PHOTOSHOP

For the most precise adjustments to tonal range, use the Curves command in Photoshop to edit the gamma curve. With the Curves dialog box open, position the cursor over the part of the scanned image you want to adjust—for example a dark area where detail is unclear—press and hold down the mouse button and a circle will appear on the Curves plot to mark the brightness of the pixel you have touched. You can then move the curve up or down at that point to change the brightness of that pixel and all others of the same tone. Moving any point on the Gamma curve will bend the entire curve, but you can isolate the point you want to move by placing a point on either side of it, so your move effects a limited range. The Curves graph can be set to display in either percentage mode (with light values on the left) or in brightness mode (with light values on the right). An "S" curve (in percentage mode) will increase contrast in an image by darkening the shadows and lightening the highlights.

By using Levels or Curves or both, you should be able to improve the tonal range of any scanned photograph or object so that its shadows are suitably dark, its highlights are bright, and its midtones have enough range and contrast so that details in these areas are clear.

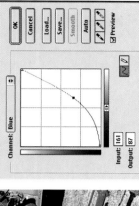
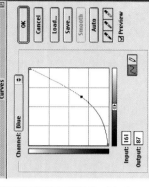

Editing midrange values with Curves controls

A dark, unedited scan of the Northern California coast produces a straight-line gamma curve in the Curves dialog box (indicating a one-to-one correlation between input and output values before editing) (**A**) and a histogram with pixels distributed toward the dark and light ends of the input brightness scale in the Levels dialog box, but not much information in the midtone range (**B**). Bending the gamma curve toward the upper left redistributes some pixels toward the midrange (**C**), improving clarity in the muddy areas. The new distribution of pixels is shown in the histogram of the edited image (**D**).

CORRECTING COLOR BALANCE

When scans are made for the reproduction of fine art—such as paintings by Van Gogh, for example—color correction and system calibration are crucial. But for most desktop publishers, the aim of color correction is to produce an image that is "pleasing" but not necessarily "accurate" (unless you are trying to match Pantone colors, for example, or exactly match an original photo). Color correction combined with calibration is even less critical for images that will be viewed only on-screen, since the digital RGB image will not have to be translated to another medium. Overall, the goal of color correction is to produce a color balance that looks natural for the subject, unless a special effect is being used deliberately.

CORRECTING SCANS USED AS FINAL ART

The type of scan and its end use will dictate color correction to a certain extent. Obviously, scanned photographs should be corrected in both tonal range and color so that they look as much like the original as possible, or else better! The same applies to a scan of an actual object placed on a scanner. In this case the scanner is acting as a camera and the resulting image should be color-corrected just as a scanned photograph would be—for example, to eliminate any color cast that may be inherent in the scanner.

CORRECTING SCANS USED AS VISUAL REFERENCES

On the other hand, when a scan is to be used as a visual photo reference or as a template for PostScript drawing, the requirements are different. Tonal and color balance need not be "correct" but should be appropriate to bring out the details that are of interest. For example, if you are planning to trace over a photograph of a dark object (such as the black swan on page 50) you will probably need to increase the contrast and brightness of the shadows and midtones to exaggerate the shapes and edges of the object so that they can be clearly seen and traced. Getting good contrast and clear edge shapes will be more important than accuracy of color in this case.

The Color Balance command in Photoshop can be used for generalized color changes, and the Variations command provides a display of a number of different color correction alternatives. But precise color correction is best done using either the Curves, Hue/Saturation, Replace Color, or Selective Color commands.

METHODS OF COLOR CORRECTION

CURVES

The Curves dialog box, as we've seen, makes it possible to change the midtone levels of an image without greatly affecting the shadows or highlights. This will not only improve midtone range (essentially the light and dark values of an image) but will also improve color balance. For example, by improving contrast in a muddy area of green, the Curves controls are actually decreasing the amount of red in the RGB mix in that area, so that the green looks more clear. The Curves dialog box can be especially effective for removing a color cast if you increase or decrease the amount of color in each of the three channels independently.

Color correction with Curves

Bending the gamma curve to the right in the Blue channel decreases the amount of blue in the image, thus removing a bluish color cast from this photo of shiny red and green tractors at a county fair.

Using Hue/Saturation controls

The tonal range was fairly good in this photo of flower-filled window boxes, but the color of the flowers and foliage was washed out. To beef up the color, Photoshop's Hue/Saturation controls were used to increase the saturation by a value of 30, which made all the colors brighter and richer.

HUE/SATURATION

Hue, saturation and brightness are characteristics used to define color and are related to the color model called HSL (defined as hue, saturation and lightness). *Hue* refers to the wavelength of a color, or, in more common terms, its name (for example, red, orange or purple). *Saturation* refers to the amount of gray in a color, with 100% saturation meaning no gray at all. *Brightness* measures the lightness or darkness of a color. Any color can be described in terms of these three parameters, and Photoshop's Hue/Saturation controls make it possible to edit color by changing the values of any or all of these parameters. The Hue/Saturation controls are especially useful for shifting the entire palette of an image (changing a green paisley design to a red one, for example) or for boosting color saturation in photos that are overexposed or faded.

REPLACE COLOR

The Replace Color controls make it possible to use color sampling dropper tools to select color areas in an image and then edit only the selected colors using Hue/Saturation controls. Replace Color is useful for editing photos in which a single element (the color of a hat, for example) needs to be changed, without affecting the colors in the rest of the image.

SELECTIVE COLOR

Selective Color is an especially powerful and useful tool for color correction of scanned photos. This command makes it possible to enhance colors in an intuitive way to produce images that may actually look better, or more ideal, than the originals. Within the Selective Color dialog box, you can independently change the CMYK components of nine separate color groups (reds, yellows, greens, cyans, blues, magentas, whites, neutrals and blacks). Through careful changes to selected color groups, many of the vicissitudes of nature and photography can be overcome, making it possible to add deep blue to what was really an overcast sky, for example, or add rich green to a parched lawn.

Using Replace Color

We wanted to change the color of the fairy's wings and leotard from pink to purple without changing her skin tones, scarf or the surrounding foliage. We opened the Replace Color dialog box, clicked on the pink color areas in the image and adjusted the Fuzziness control to create a mask. Then when we moved the Hue slider in the Transform section of the dialog box, only the selected pink areas were affected.

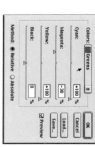

Using Selective Color

This photo of an Italian vegetable market needed finely tuned color correction to different areas—the red tomatoes had a slightly bluish cast and were too saturated, while the green beans and lettuce were a little washed out. To improve the photo we used Selective Color to independently edit the CMYK components of the reds, greens, yellows and whites which added richness and warmth without greatly affecting the overall brightness or contrast of the image.

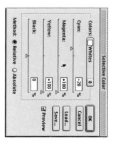

Crafting Quality Images

CLEANUP AND REPAIR

One of the most exciting things about working with scanned photographs is that many of the problems that plague photographers—from scratches on prints to unwanted elements in a composition—can be fixed or eliminated using image-editing tools.

GETTING RID OF SPECKS

Dust on a negative leaves specks on a photo print, and these will show up when the photo is scanned. Likewise, dust or scratches on the scanner glass will leave specks on the scan. Large blips can be smoothed over by hand by using a smudge, blur or rubber stamp tool. But Photoshop's Dust & Scratches filter works wonderfully well to clean up an entire image in one pass, and it can be adjusted to search for and eliminate specks of different sizes. Be aware though that this filter will blur an image, resulting in loss of sharpness and detail.

REPAIRING DAMAGE

Old photographs, or roughly used new ones, often have white cracks or gaps caused by folding or tearing. It's possible to restore scans of damaged photos by using Photoshop's rubber stamp tool to sample adjacent areas and paint over the flaws. The key to seamless photo restoration is to paint with similar texture areas. Simply smudging or blurring an area is not always enough, as it can create sections of flat color that look unnatural. Look for areas that are similar in texture as well as tone to the area you're repairing and take your samples from these areas, even if they are not near the area of damage.

REMOVING EXTRANEOUS DETAILS

Sometimes you've got a great photograph except that there's a telephone pole growing out of the subject's head. When objects in the background appear to be connected to objects in the foreground in a distracting way, it's called *merging*. There are at least two ways to deal with this problem in Photoshop. Use the rubber stamp tool to sample an adjacent area of the photo and then paint over the offending object with this sample. Or, select the background and blur it or reduce its contrast or color saturation so that it appears to recede farther into the distance.

Repairing an old photo
A 1950s print of two young tap dancers was cracked, torn and taped together. To eliminate the cracks and marks we used the rubber stamp tool to sample adjacent areas and carefully paint over the flaws. (The same method can be used to remove the stains that often appear on old photos.) We then improved the contrast using Levels, and sharpened the focus using Unsharp Mask.

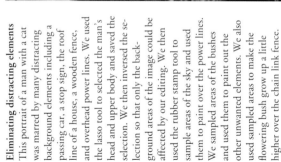

Eliminating distracting elements
This portrait of a man with a cat was marred by many distracting background elements including a passing car, a stop sign, the roof line of a house, a wooden fence, and overhead power lines. We used the lasso tool to selected the man's head and upper body and saved the selection. We then inversed the selection so that only the background areas of the image could be affected by our editing. We then used the rubber stamp tool to sample areas of the sky and used them to paint over the power lines. We sampled areas of the bushes and used them to paint out the other unwanted elements. We also used sampled areas to make the flowering bush grow up a little higher over the chain link fence.

For more examples of this kind of image editing see "Altering and Enhancing Scanned Photos" starting on page 76.

Silhouetting an object

The key to silhouetting is to use the tool or technique that makes it easiest to select the background elements you want to delete. Sometimes it's necessary to use several selection techniques on a single image, since background characteristics can vary at different locations around the image. To silhouette an accordion player (**A**), we started by trying the Color Range command to see if we could use it to select just the green parts of the background. But unfortunately, this function also selected the yellow areas of the

accordion (**B**). So instead we used the magic wand tool, set at a relatively high tolerance of 64 pixels, to click around the edges of the figure, which selected much of the background (**C**). We used the polygon lasso to select and delete most of the background (**D**). But we used Photoshop's new Extract command to select the wispy areas of hair on the right side of the face (**E**) To silhouette the rough edges left behind by the Extract command (**F**) we painted along the edges of the hair with a soft white brush (**G**) to produce the final silhouetted image (**H**).

REMOVING BACKGROUNDS

Objects in nature never appear without a context. But one of the great strengths (and weaknesses) of human intelligence is our ability to isolate an object from its surroundings, both visually and intellectually. This is expressed graphically by the *vignette* or *silhouette*, in which an object stands alone without its background. Silhouetted objects can make dramatic focal points for a composition or can be used as elements in a collage. A silhouetted object is also easier to trace by hand when using a photo as a visual reference (see "Creating and Editing 'Photo Scrap'" on page 48).

USING SELECTION TOOLS

There are a variety of ways to silhouette an object in Photoshop. We recommend that you practice each one (or the similar tools found in other image-editing programs) to develop your skill and a feel for which tools are best suited to the demands of different types of images. Selection can be tricky, but it's one of the most powerful functions available in an image-editing program.

USING THE LASSO TOOLS

The simple **lasso tool** in Photoshop can be used to draw freehand along the edges of an object to create a selection outline around it. However it can be awkward to do this accurately using the mouse, so you may prefer using the **polygon lasso** to click from point to point along the edges of an object. Even when selecting a curved object, the series of short line segments made with the polygon lasso will do a good job of approximating the curve. The **magnetic lasso** tool will automatically snap-to and place a point along the strongest edges in an image; that is, the areas of greatest contrast. This tool can be used to automate the lasso selection process somewhat, though the points may not always be placed where you intend them to be.

USING THE PEN TOOLS

Similar to the polygon lasso, the **pen tool** creates selection outlines when you click from point to point, but the points created by the pen tool are PostScript Bezier anchor points that can be manipulated to change the slope of the line segments and to create curves between any two points. There is also a **magnetic pen** which places anchor points automatically along high contrast boundaries.

USING THE MAGIC WAND TOOL

Clicking in an area with the **magic wand** will select all the contiguous pixels of the same color (or range of colors), depending on the tonal range (tolerance) that you have specified. The wand can be used to automatically select large areas of background, which can then be deleted. In addition, the contiguous mode can be turned off so that the wand selects all tones in the specified range throughout the image.

*One must be as clear as one's natural
reticence allows one to be.*
—Marianne Moore, 1953

B

A

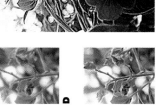

C

D

F

E

USING THE MAGIC ERASER

This tool works in a way similar to the magic wand, but when you click with the **magic eraser** on a tonal area you want to eliminate, it both selects and deletes all pixels of that tonal range with one click. It can be set to select pixels that are contiguous or that occur throughout an image.

SELECTING BY COLOR RANGE

The **Color Range** command makes it possible to select tonal areas in a way similar to the magic wand, but with more control. A dialog box includes an image area which lets you see how the selection area is being built up as you click on the image to indicate the color areas you want included in the selection.

USING THE EXTRACT COMMAND

New in Photoshop 5.5, the **Extract** command makes it possible for you to use the mouse to define where the boundaries of your object are. This is done by dragging an "edge highlighter" around the part of an image you want to silhouette. After defining the edge, a preview lets you see the selection outline that's been created, before committing to it. This function is especially good for selecting fine edges such as the branches of a tree or wisps of hair.

USING THE BACKGROUND ERASER

The brush area of the **background eraser** includes a "hot spot" that samples the color under it and a surrounding area in which all pixels of similar color will be erased (depending on the parameters you set) as you drag the brush.

For more detailed information on making selections and modifying them, see the manual for your image-editing software. For Photoshop users we highly recommend *The Photoshop Wow! Book* series by Linnea Dayton and Jack Davis (Peachpit Press).

SHARPENING IMAGES

Image-editing programs like Photoshop provide various filters for sharpening images to improve focus. These work by first analyzing the image for adjacent light and dark pixels that represent an "edge" and then increasing the contrast along the edge (making the darks darker and the lights lighter) to heighten focus. This process works fairly well, and in fact a similar "sharpen" filter is built into our eyes (it's called "lateral inhibition") to accentuate borders in our visual field. Unfortunately, a standard sharpen filter will sharpen everything in an image, including dust, scratches and speckled areas. A "sharpen edges" filter is an improvement, as it sharpens only edges with larger tonal differences. But the most useful sharpening process is curiously called unsharp masking, and the Unsharp Mask filter in Photoshop additionally provides controls for adapting the filter to the needs of particular images.

The process of unsharp masking, both conventional and digital, provides high contrast along edges without disturbing the contrast in areas of smoother gradation.

WHAT IS UNSHARP MASK?

Unsharp mask has its unlikely name because it's the digital analogue of a process with the same name that began in the photographic darkroom. To sharpen the edges in the four negatives made in the traditional color separation process, the original color transparency (a positive image) is used to produce an out-of-focus, low-contrast negative called an unsharp mask. This negative is placed over the color transparency as each of the four separation negatives is made. The unsharp mask affects the amount of light reaching the negative film for each color and tends to exaggerate the edges in the image. This happens because dark areas of the transparency are exposed to more light (darkened) because they are covered by light areas of the mask, while light areas of the transparency are exposed to less light (lightened) because they are protected by dark areas of the mask.

Sharpening an image

A photo of flowers was taken in low light and suffers from a shallow depth of field and lack of focus (**A**). We applied the Sharpen More (**B**) filter, which did not do a very good job of improving the focus. We then experimented with different settings for the Unsharp Mask filter and found that values of Amount 150, Radius 2, Threshold 0 produced a good result (**C**). Close-up shots show the difference before (**D**) and after (**E**) using Unsharp Mask. Setting the Unsharp Mask filter at values that are too high can produce a halo effect, but sometimes this distorted sharpening is interesting as a special effect (**F**).

Photoshop's Unsharp Mask filter provides three controls: Amount determines the intensity of the filter; Radius controls how many pixels around each sample pixel (the contrast "halo") will be analyzed; and Threshold determines the amount of difference between adjacent pixels needed to define them as an edge. Experimenting and learning to set these parameters makes it possible to sharpen images effectively without unwanted side effects such as an exaggerated halo effect, stairstepping of pixels along hard edges, or speckling. Publications on scanning, including *Real World Scanning and Halftones, 2nd Edition* by David Blatner, Glenn Fleishman and Steve Roth (Peachpit Press, 1998), provide detailed information on adjusting the Unsharp Mask filter to get the best results. It's best to save sharpening as one of the last operations in image-editing, since it can exaggerate any flaws in the image. Also, be aware that Unsharp Mask slightly increases the contrast in an image.

ELIMINATING MOIRÉ PATTERNS

Photographic prints and art such as drawings and paintings scan well because their surfaces are composed of continuous tones. But a *print* produced by offset lithography (such as a photo reproduced in a book or magazine) has been converted to a halftone screen for printing and contains tiny dots in a grid, which can produce a distracting moiré pattern when the print is scanned. This happens because the dot screen of the halftone can interfere with the dot screen imposed by the scanning process. With a digital scan of a half-toned image there are actually two possibilities for interference—between the halftone screen of the original and the dot screen of the scanner, and between the screen of the original and the screen of the output device when the scan is printed.

Moiré patterns can be reduced in a number of ways. Photoshop's Despeckle filter will remove some of the patterning and the Unsharp Mask filter can be used afterward to carefully restore the focus. The Median filter used at a low setting offers more control and its effects can also be corrected later with Unsharp Mask.

Another way to reduce moiré patterning is to scan the original at a resolution about four times higher than the final resolution you need, apply the Despeckle, Median, or Blur filter to soften the pattern, and then resample it down to your desired resolution. When working on a moiré pattern, pay most attention to how the image looks on the screen at a 1:1 ratio. You may see a moiré pattern at other ratios because of interference between the screen frequency of the original and the dot grid of your monitor, but this will not show up when the image is printed.

Although moiré patterns can be reduced through careful editing, the appearance of a moiré pattern should always prompt the question, "Am I scanning copyrighted material?" Most printed images are covered by copyright protection (see "Copyright Issues" on pages 27–28).

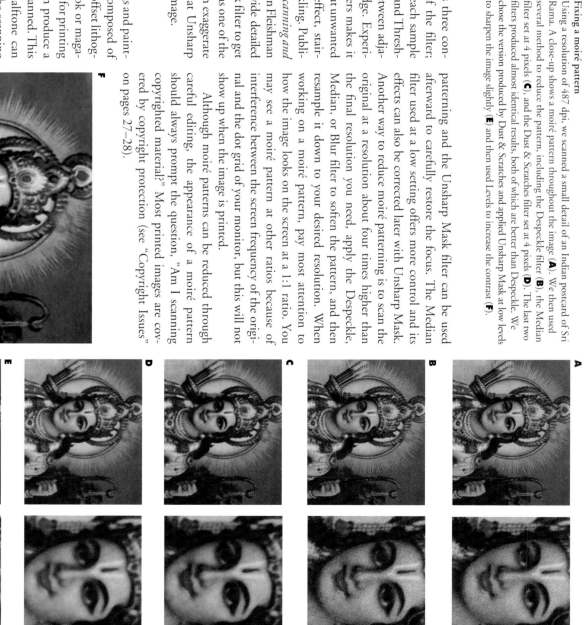

Fixing a moiré pattern
Using a resolution of 487 dpi, we scanned a small detail of an Indian postcard of Sri Rama. A close-up shows a moiré pattern throughout the image (**A**). We then used several method to reduce the pattern, including the Despeckle filter (**B**), the Median filter set at 4 pixels (**C**), and the Dust & Scratches filter set at 4 pixels (**D**). The last two filters produced almost identical results, both of which are better than Despeckle. We chose the version produced by Dust & Scratches and applied Unsharp Mask at low levels to sharpen the image slightly (**E**) and then used Levels to increase the contrast (**F**).

5 Working with Printed Clip Art

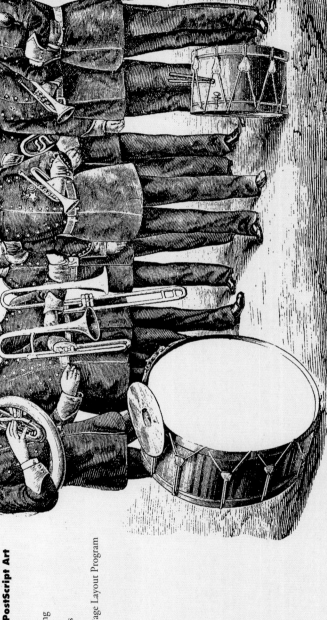

Finding the Right Picture

SOURCES OF PRINTED CLIP ART

Where do you turn when you need an image to decorate a newsletter or brochure and don't have the time or the budget for a custom illustration? Try scanning some of the thousands of high-quality images in the "public domain." There's only one catch: to have an expired copyright an image must be at least 75 years old. An historic illustration can look fresh and modern though if it's used with contemporary type and other design elements. In other instances, the retro look may be just what your design calls for. We'll explore the most accessible sources of copyright-free art and describe how you can obtain it, scan it, and alter it to fit your needs.

PRINTED ARCHIVAL ART COLLECTIONS

Dover Publications, based in New York City, publishes over 700 books in their Pictorial Archives series, containing over 250,000 copyright-free illustrations. These are printed in both black-and-white and color and include advertising cuts; botanical drawings; quilt and embroidery patterns; stencil designs; European, Asian, African, South American and Native American ornament; collections of symbols; folk art; architectural renderings; historical engravings; alphabets; and much more. This art has been culled from old, out-of-print books dating from the Middle Ages through the early 20th century, though most of it is drawn from the early advertising art produced around the turn of the last century. Because most of the art predates the camera, it consists mainly of black-and-white line drawings and engravings, though Dover does publish some collections of early black-and-white photographs. Dover has done the work of scouring old book stores and libraries for copyright-free art and has assembled it in an accessible form: inexpensive paperback books containing clearly printed black-and-white art, arranged by subject matter

The Dover Pictorial Archives

The art reproduced by Dover in its Pictorial Archives series ranges from the Renaissance to the 1920s. The illustrations shown here include a botanical woodcut of a ginger plant from Heck's *Pictorial Archive of Nature and Science* (Dover, 1994), and a 1920s Italian illustration of two men from *Treasury of Book Ornament and Decoration* (Dover, 1986). Both illustrations are clear, simple black-and-white line drawings which will reproduce well as bit-mapped scans. Art such as the Italian illustration, characterized by heavier areas of black, can also be effectively autotraced and converted to Post-Script format (see techniques on page 36). However, much of Dover's clip art is taken from 19th Century engravings like the reaper from *1800 Woodcuts by Thomas Bewick and His School* (Dover, 1962).

and available either by mail order or at local art supply stores. "Period" art like that collected by Dover can add a special flavor to contemporary publications and is often used in collage illustrations. But sometimes a contemporary look is needed, so Dover also publishes a smaller number of current, copyright-free clip art, containing simple, easy-to-reproduce illustrations drawn especially for them. The artistic quality of these illustrations is not as high as that of the older art, but it can often serve as a good starting point for an illustration. Other publishers also offer books of "scan-able" clip art. Take a look at the book selection at your local art supply store or search on the Internet.

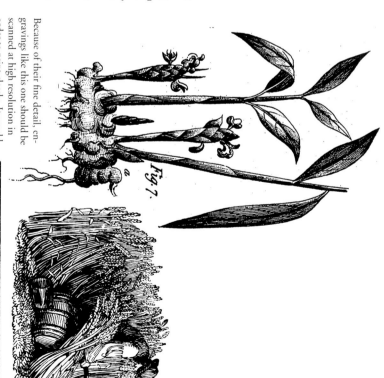

Because of their fine detail, engravings like this one should be scanned at high resolution in order to print clearly. It would be possible to autotrace a scanned engraving, but the autotracing would produce a file containing small shapes with many anchor points and might prove cumbersome to print. All three illustrations shown here were printed from TIFF files scanned at 300 dpi.

Fig. 7.

QUICK TIP

To prevent show-through when scanning from a book with pages printed on both sides, place a piece of black paper behind the page you're placing face down on your scanner.

Alligator from *1800 Woodcuts by Thomas Bewick and His School* (Dover, 1962)

GOVERNMENT SOURCES

The Library of Congress contains many old manuscripts and has a service that provides photographic reproductions of illustrations taken from these books. The Library charges a fee for the photos, but in most cases there is no fee for use of the image. Many other government libraries, including the National Library of Medicine, also provide this service and will send you a price list of illustrations that are currently available.

OLD BOOKS WITH EXPIRED COPYRIGHTS

If you have the time and inclination to probe further, you can go directly to the original sources. Wander through used book stores or through the shelves of a large library, especially university libraries. Books published 75 years before the current date should be in the public domain, though copyright law is complex and changing. The Copyright law of 1909 made it possible to copyright work for 28 years, and renew the copyright for another 28 years, for a total of 56 years. But Congress found that the requirement for a specific renewal process was often difficult for widows and orphans of deceased artists and many valuable works fell into the public domain to the detriment of the creator's heirs. The law now states that works created after 1978 are automatically protected for the lifetime of the author plus 50 years, with no requirement for renewal. For works created before 1978, copyrights can live out their first 28-year term and be renewed for an additional 47 years, for a total of 75 years of copyright protection.

COPYRIGHT ISSUES

Copyright protects photos and artwork (as well as writing, music, films and other works) so that their author (or other assigned copyright holder) controls their reproduction. Anyone else must ask permission to repro-

Government sources of art
This woodcut of a Renaissance birth stool is taken from midwifery textbook published in Germany in 1513. We ordered it as an 8 by 10-inch glossy photographic print (Neg. No. 66-493) from the National Library of Medicine.

Art from out-of-print books
This printer's dingbat, type ornament, and initial S are taken from the back cover of a handmade book published in 1906 by Elbert Hubbard of The Roycrofters press in East Aurora, New York. The Roycrofters books are still admired as fine examples of letterpress printing in the craftsman style. The entire back cover design is reproduced on page 29.

ART FOR FREE (OR ALMOST FREE)
SOURCES OF COPYRIGHT-FREE PRINTED CLIP ART
Here are some good sources of copyright-free illustration, ornament and typography.

DOVER PUBLICATIONS
31 East 2nd Street
Mineola, NY 11501
Write to request a copy of Dover's Pictorial Archives catalog of copyright-free art. Dover does not accept credit card orders or orders by telephone or fax.

LIBRARY OF CONGRESS
Prints & Photos Division
Independent Avenue at First Street, SE
Washington DC, 20540
202/707-6394
www.loc.gov

THE SMITHSONIAN INSTITUTION
Eighth and P Streets, NW
Washington, DC 20560
202/357-1886,
202/786-2563 fax
www.si.edu

BOOKS IN THE PUBLIC DOMAIN
Most books published at least 75 years before the current date are in the public domain.

SUBJECT COLLECTIONS
Compiled by Lee Ash and W. G. Miller
Published by R. R. Bowker
www.bowker.com
This library reference book is a "guide to special book collections and subject emphases as reported by university, college, public and special libraries in museums in the United States and Canada." Use it to find sources of old books on specific topics.

Engraving, then, is, in brief terms, the Art of Scratch.
—John Ruskin, 1873

duce a copyrighted work and must often pay a fee for its use. Copyright law protects artists from misuse or exploitation of their work. The notion behind the law is that the person who labors to create an original work should reap whatever tangible rewards come from its use. So using someone else's work without permission is like sneaking into your neighbor's garden at night to pick their tomatoes. It is a form of stealing. The purpose of the copyright law is clear enough, but new technologies make it increasingly easy to violate copyright laws and get away with it. Just as home CD "burners" make it easy to copy a friend's new music CD, so desktop scanners make it easy to capture and use copyrighted images. Most of us would agree that scanning an original photo or drawing and reprinting it unaltered without permission is a blatant violation of the artist's rights. This sort of abuse is probably not very common, if only because the perpetrator is likely to get caught for reproducing a recognizable image. More subtle are the many instances in which we are tempted to scan and use *parts* of a copyrighted image and alter them so that their original source is no longer recognizable. This kind of appropriation is also illegal (in many cases) but is probably more common because it's difficult to detect. One can justify such use by arguing that in the process of alteration a new work has been created, one which is not in competition with the original. A law suit for copyright infringement is not likely if you scan an image and alter it so much that an ordinary person could not detect that your version was derived from the original. In the end, the appropriate use of scanning technology involves judgments based on a number of ethical, legal, aesthetic and practical factors in which our desire to be honest and honorable is balanced against expedience.

MAKING IT WORK

USING SCANNED ART IN YOUR LAYOUT

Clip art from historical sources can work well in contemporary designs. For example, use a simple, modern type treatment to set off the detail of an early engraving. Or contrast an elegant image from the early 20th century with a older, serif typeface. We used the four images on these two pages to create designs for (from left) a tea bag, a business card, a CD cover, and a booklet page. The fifth example is a version of the original Roycrofters book cover, edited to remove the dark brown background of the original.

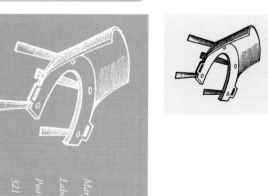

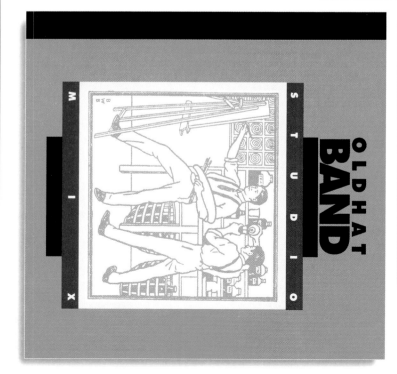

Introduction

Americans want comfortable, attractive, functional, and durable housing. Yet, many increasingly find high quality housing beyond their means. Conventional building methods rely on plentiful resources. With some of these resources dwindling, housing costs are sky rocketing. The cost of a home includes materials, construction, financing, taxes, energy consumption, and insurance. This booklet explores recent attempts to reduce those costs. Construction techniques discussed in this booklet focus on building resource-efficient and energy-conserving homes, without sacrificing affordability or quality.

In a cooperative demonstration project between the U.S. Department of Energy (DOE), the U.S. Department of Housing and Urban Development (HUD), and the Navajo Nation, current home designs on the Navajo reservation were evaluated and recommendations were made to improve quality and lower the costs. The resulting design utilized straw-bale wall construction.

Straw-bale building is a practical and perhaps under utilized construction method. Initiated in the United States at the turn of the century, straw-bale building is showing new merit in today's marketplace. Walls of straw, easily constructed and structurally sound, promise to take some of the pressure off of limited forest resources.

Straw is a viable building alternative, plentiful and inexpensive. Straw-bale buildings boast superinsulated walls (R-50), simple construction, low costs, and the conversion of an agricultural byproduct into a valued building material. Properly constructed and maintained, the straw-bale walls, stucco exterior and plaster interior remain water proof, fire resistant, and pest free. Because only limited skill is required, a community house-raising effort can build most of a straw-bale house in a single day. This effort yields a low-cost, elegant, and energy-efficient living space for the owners, a graceful addition to the community, and a desirable boost to local farm income. This booklet offers an in-depth look at one such community house-raising, in addition to a general overview of straw-bale construction.

Working with Bitmapped Images

MODIFYING SCANNED ART IN AN IMAGE-EDITING PROGRAM

Scanned clip art can be transformed in a variety of ways, using a "paint" or image-editing program such as Photoshop or Painter. Such programs make it possible to add color to black-and-white art and also to change the colors of scanned color art (see the sections on using color on pages 32–34). In addition, image-editing programs can be used to alter the scanned image to fit your needs and space constraints—for example, by deleting parts of it, or by cropping or silhouetting an image.

Images produced with image-editing software are bitmaps, so choose a resolution that suits your purpose. Images that will be used "on-screen" (for a CD-ROM presentation or a home page for the World Wide Web, for example) can be created at the relatively low screen resolution of 72 dpi. But low-resolution art that is printed at very large sizes will look jagged, especially on diagonal edges. For a smoother result, especially when printing bitmaps to film for four-color process printing, we've found it's best to use a resolution about 1.67 times the final printed line screen (see "Getting the Most Out of Your Scanner" on page 11).

CROPPING, DELETING, INVERTING, SCALING AND OTHER TRANSFORMATIONS

One of the easiest ways to modify scanned clip art is to crop it to emphasize a particular figure or part. Another easy modification is to delete parts of an illustration so that a central feature is silhouetted. Image-editing programs also include functions for rotating, skewing, flipping and scaling art. Turn to "Flipping, Rotating and Skewing" (page 40) to see examples of how these transformations can be used to alter clip art.

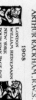

Using a detail
To isolate a rambling berry bush engraved by Arthur Rackham from a scan of a 1908 title page, we cropped to the main engraving and then used the eraser tool in Photoshop to delete the background hills and the moon. The finished art was used on a soda can label.

Playing with negatives
Reversing an image from positive to negative can give it new meaning. For a flyer, we started with a 1700s woodcut of a sun from *1800 Woodcuts by Thomas Bewick and His School* (Dover, 1962). We covered one half of the image to the negative to suggest a transition from day to night. A headline in a modern sans serif typeface brings the old image into the 21st century. A color fade background and a truck from Object Gear photo clip art complete the design.

Scanning in gray scale
The fine detail of the original 19th century engraving (from *Music: A Pictorial Archive of Woodcuts and Engravings* (Dover, 1980) is captured in a scan made in grayscale mode (256 gray levels) at 600 dpi.

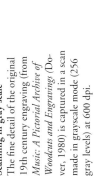

WORKING WITH SCANNED ENGRAVINGS

During the 19th century the technique of the steel-point engraving was perfected. Characteristic of these prints are the thousands of black undulating parallel lines that follow the shapes of the forms being modeled. They are often met by a set of white lines running at a different angle. Using tools with multiple tips, the engravers subtly changed the pressure as they scribed, causing variations in tone. Unlike the uniform mechanical screening of a halftone, the engravers used different textures for each part of the image. Using scans of reproduction of these engravings requires some special editing care.

SCAN AS GRAYSCALE FIRST

To bring out the exquisite detail in this line art we recommend scanning first in 256 shades of gray, rather than in black-and-white only. In an image-editing program, set the contrast to maximum (**A**). Then experiment with increasing (**B**), or decreasing (**C**) the brightness until the line detail is optimal. Alternatively, try using the adjustments to contrast and midtones described on pages 16–18, "Improving Image Quality."

A (In Photoshop) contrast Increased 100% and saved as a bitmap

B Contrast increased 100% and brightness decreased 50%

C Contrast increased 100% and brightness increased 15%

What a joyous thing is color! How influenced we all are by it, even if we are unconscious of how our sense of restfulness has been brought about.
—Elsie De Wolfe, 1920

USING COLOR WHEELS AND PALETTES

Combining colors in a pleasing way is a skill based on good aesthetic judgment and an intuitive eye. But we can be guided by the centuries-old device of the color wheel to find combinations of hues that work well together. The most basic color wheel consists of the three primary pigments (red, blue and yellow) and the three secondary pigments (orange, purple and green), arranged around a circle in the order they appear in the rainbow (below, left). Color wheels can also be subdivided to produce a larger palette, as in our 12-color wheel (below, right). We have further divided our wheel into tints (50%) and shades (add 15% black) of the original colors (bottom). By choosing color pairs or groups that are related to each other, you can reliably produce color combinations that are harmonious. The illustrations on these two pages were colored primarily with hues chosen from these three color wheels.

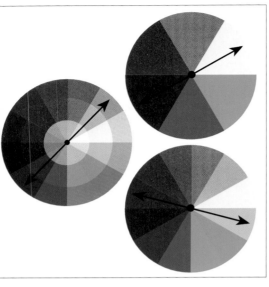

Starting with black and white
To create line art for our color studies we scanned a decorative tiled pattern from *Treasury of Book Ornament and Decoration* (Dover, 1986). In Photoshop we deleted all but one pair of birds and combined the upper and lower tree elements to create an illustration. We then autotraced the image to produce a PostScript graphic and opened it in Illustrator to add type and an arched background.

Complementary color pairs
Complements are colors that lie directly across from each other on a color wheel. These color "opposites" can be used effectively together but their strong contrast sometimes produces a shimmering effect. To avoid trapping problems between color complements (white gaps between solid color areas) edit each color so that it includes at least a small percentage of cyan, magenta and yellow.

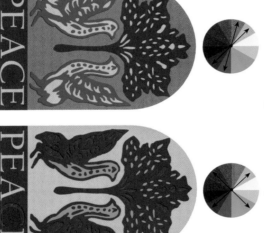

Double complements
Double complements are pairs of complements which can be combined to produce a palette of four colors that look good together.

Near complements
Near complements are the two colors that lie on either side of a complement. So, for example, the near complements of green are the red-orange and red-purple that lie on either side of green's complement, red. Near complement groups produce especially harmonious combinations.

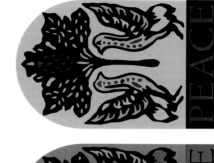

Pastel variations
Most color wheels show fully saturated rainbow hues. But using these as a guide, you can produce effective color combinations using tints. Shown here are a near complement group of tints (left) and the same group with one of the hues at full saturation (right).

Triadic complements
Triadic complements are groups of three colors that lie equidistant from each other around a color wheel.

Multiple complements
Multiple complements are groups of three, four or five colors that are adjacent to each other on a color wheel.

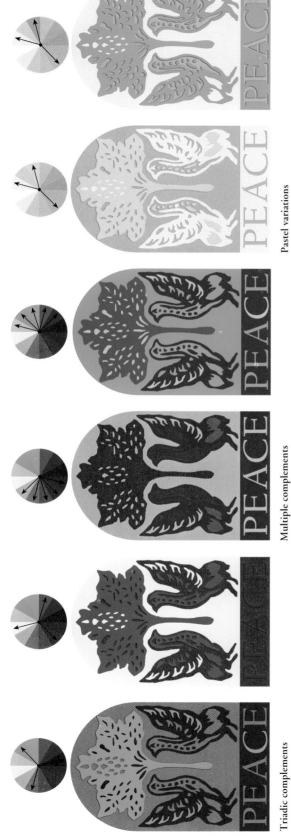

Using muted tones
Create muted process colors by adding black (wheel at left), or add "gray" by increasing black and reducing cyan, magenta and yellow (wheel at right). At left, two muted colors are combined with gray. At right, muted multiple complements are combined.

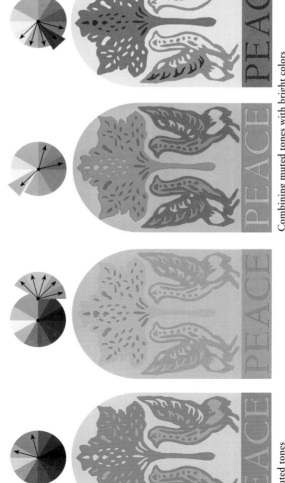

Setting off brights and neutrals with black
Once you've determined an effective color combination, try using black to give it even more power. Black can be used to set off bright color combinations (left) and produces a handsome palette when combined with neutral shades of brown or gray and bright accent colors (right).

Combining muted tones with bright colors
Combining muted tones with fully saturated accent colors is an especially effective combination. We used muted near complements with bright gold (left) and muted multiple complements with bright red (right).

ADDING COLOR

Most clip art is created and printed in black-and-white. But color can be added to scanned clip art in a variety of ways. For printed projects, the easiest way to add one color is to incorporate scanned black-and-white art into an electronic or traditional layout and ask your printer to print it in a color ink. Or, to easily add a second color, print on colored paper. For "on-screen" projects or full-color printing you can add color electronically by opening a black-and-white scanned image in an image-editing program and filling the black and white areas with different colors.

A

B

C

Coloring artwork

To add color to a simple black-and-white design, we scanned a stylized graphic of a Japanese woman serving tea, opened it in Photoshop and filled the black areas with dark blue and the white areas with a very pale green. The finished two-color image could be printed either in two colors on white paper or in one color on colored paper (**A**). The image was taken from *Graphic Trade Symbols by German Designers* (Dover, 1974).

To vary a one-color treatment, we used various tints of dark blue to fill different areas of the image. The tints were achieved in Photoshop by filling selected areas with the original dark purple color at varying percentages of opacity (**B**). A three-color design was created in the same way by filling areas with both tints and solids of three different hues—blue, green and turquoise (**C**).

In the original black-and-white image, the woman's hair, kimono and the background are continuous with the round black border. To separate these areas from each other, we drew lines between them using the line tool loaded with white paint (**D**). We then added colors to create a full-color version and imported the bitmap into Illustrator to create a poster (**E**).

D

Creating color variations

Once you have created art in full color, either by scanning a color original or by adding color to scanned black-and-white art, you can change the palette by using an image-editing program to change the hue or saturation of the entire image. We used Photoshop's Hue/Saturation controls to shift the hues in our full-color tea graphic (**F**). It's also interesting to experiment with painting lighter colors into areas of the black-and-white original that were black and dark colors into areas that were white (**G**).

JAPANESE

·Green·Tea·

16 TEA BAGS   NET WT 1 OZ

E

F

G

USING FILTERS ON LINE ART

The various filters that image-editing programs provide for transforming images (such as Sharpen, Find Edges, Blur and so on) were developed for use with scanned continuous-tone photographs. But it's possible to get interesting and useful effects by experimenting with these filters on scanned line art. We've had the best results when applying filters to fairly simple images that have thick or rough strokes, as opposed to those with many fine lines, such as old engravings. Our demonstration image of a drummer was scanned from *Old-Fashioned Music Illustrations* (Dover, 1990), part of the Dover Clip-Art Series. The filter effects shown here were created in Photoshop.

Artistic, Neon Glow

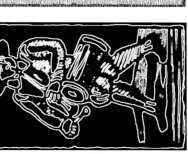

Pixelate, Pointillize

Texture, Texturizer

Artistic, Fresco

Pixelate, Mezzotint

Stylize, Glowing Edges

Artistic, Colored Pencil

Distort, Diffuse Glow

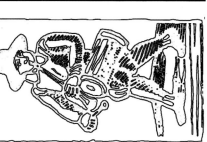

Stylize, Find Edges

Original image

Brush Strokes, Angled Strokes

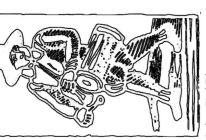

Stylize, Emboss

Artistic, Rough Pastels

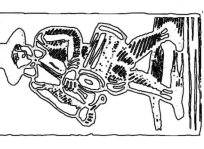

Sketch, Water Paper

Artistic, Plastic Wrap

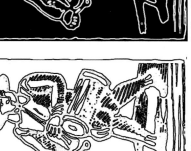

Sketch, Note Paper

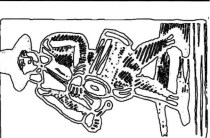

Converting Bitmaps to PostScript Art

AUTOTRACING

Editing scanned clip art in a program like Photoshop can produce wonderful effects, especially of the "painterly" kind, but bitmapped images must be scanned and printed at high resolutions (usually 250 dpi and above) to look smooth. Converting scanned clip art to PostScript format produces smaller, more compact files and makes it possible to print at any size with the same smooth resolution. This is especially useful when art will be used in a business identity package with many differently sized components (see pages 44-45). One way to convert a scanned image is to open it as a "template" in a PostScript illustration program such as Illustrator, FreeHand or CorelDraw and trace around the shapes with a drawing tool. But by far the easiest way to convert to PostScript is to use "autotracing."

In the *autotracing* process the outlines of a scanned image are automatically traced and converted to PostScript paths. Many PostScript illustration programs include autotracing tools. But for more control, especially with complex art, it's better to use a program like Adobe Streamline, which is dedicated to autotracing. While most autotracing is done with black-and-white line art, Streamline can also convert grayscale scans and produce posterizations (see the opposite page).

The autotracer will trace the outlines of every shape in a scan, no matter how small or extraneous, so to get good results prepare your scans beforehand by eliminating small specks and spots. The goal in autotracing is to produce a PostScript version that faithfully reproduces the scanned line art with as few paths and anchor points as possible, since overly complex PostScript files can be difficult to manage and print. Some of the necessary bitmap editing can be done in Streamline itself, or for more sophisticated changes, use an image-editing program to prepare the scan before opening it in Streamline.

D

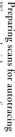

C

B

A

E

F

Preparing scans for autotracing
We started with a scan of a rose type ornament from *Old-Time Advertising Cuts and Typography: 184 Plates from the Boston Type and Stereotype Foundry Catalog (1832)* (Dover, 1974) (**A**). To open up the white areas of the image we used Levels to increase contrast and brighten the midtones. We applied the Dust & Scratches filter to eliminate stray marks and then applied Unsharp Mask to sharpen the focus (**B**). We tested for "leaks" in the image by using the paint bucket tool to dump a shade of gray into the background. We saw that the gray bled into some of the leaf and stem shapes (**C**). So we used a black brush to close the gaps in some of the lines and

finished off our preparation by painting out larger stray marks with both white and black brushes. We then opened the edited scan in Streamline and did an outline autotracing (**D**). Then, to add color, we opened the autotracing in Illustrator, selected the white shapes and filled them with color (**E**).

In outline mode Streamline converts line drawings to PostScript shapes by creating white shapes placed over a black background shape. So the black lines of the original art are defined by the areas of black that show through the gaps between the white shapes. An exploded view of the autotracing shows how the black and white shapes are layered on top of each other (**F**).

Working with colored clip art

To create art from a vintage French fashion plate scanned from a 1922 Condé Nast publication (**A**) we converted the image to grayscale mode, used Levels to increase the contrast, applied Dust & Scratches to eliminate small marks and applied Unsharp Mask at high values to exaggerate the edges of the figure (**B**). We used the Posterize command to posterize the image into four levels of tone: black, dark gray, light gray and white (**C**). We then painted with these four tones to smooth jagged areas and fill gaps in the outline of the woman's body (**D**). We then selected the areas of the image that included the fine lines of the woman's arms and head and applied the Unsharp Mask filter at levels high enough to sharpen and darken these lines (**E**). The image was now ready for autotracing in Streamline's Color/Grayscale mode at four levels of posterization (**F**). We opened the autotracing in Illustrator and added color and type to create a poster (**G**).

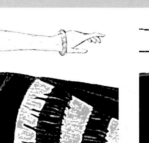
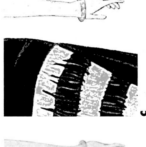
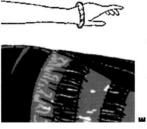
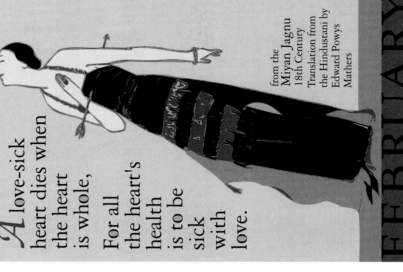

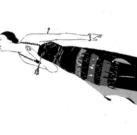

EN PLEIN COEUR
ROBE DU SOIR, DE PAUL POIRET

A

B

C

D

E

F

G

FEBRUARY

A love-sick heart dies when the heart is whole, For all the heart's health is to be sick with love.

from the
Miyan Jagnu
18th Century
Translation from
the Hindustani by
Edward Powys
Mathers

CLEANING UP SCANS

Eliminate any unwanted specks either by painting over them with a brush tool, or by using Photoshop's Dust & Scratches or Median filters, or by increasing the brightness and contrast of the entire image. Unclog black areas that have filled in by painting into them with white. Clogged black areas are especially common in reproductions of older engravings in which actual ink clogging has occurred.

ISOLATING SEPARATE AREAS

If you plan to apply different colors to different areas of the final PostScript image, separate them in the bitmap before autotracing so that separate PostScript paths are produced for each area. Otherwise, you may end up with a large and complex path that snakes its way through several elements of an image. With simple images, look by eye for places where continuous shapes should be broken and separate them by painting either a white line or a black line. For more detailed images, try pouring a color or gray into a shape that you think is separate and see if it "bleeds" color into adjacent shapes (they may be connected by a single pixel "bridge" you haven't noticed). If so, the color will immediately show you where you need to put your breaks.

SMOOTHING THE EDGES

Scanned engravings are often full of complex, jagged shapes. Autotracing these without advance editing can produce complex PostScript paths defined by hundreds of control points set close together. To get a smoother PostScript line, try blurring the scan beforehand to soften the edges of the shapes. After blurring, increase the brightness and contrast to restore a smooth edge.

ADDING COLOR

Once you have autotraced a scanned image to create PostScript shapes, color can be added easily using the same techniques as for any PostScript drawing. Shapes can be filled with solid color or with color gradations. You can apply a built-in patterned fill from the library that comes with your illustration program, or create a pattern of your own and mask it into a shape. Shapes can be filled without a "stroke" (outline) or with a stroke in a contrasting color. It is also possible to "color" an image with another image, by pasting an imported TIFF image into a PostScript shape, as for example, pasting a photograph of a piece of lace into the sails of a ship.

Another way to add color to a scanned image in a PostScript drawing program is to import it as a 1-bit TIFF image and draw colored shapes behind it that will show through the transparent areas of the TIFF. Using this technique it's possible to create a "sandwich" image that imitates the look of a hand-colored engraving (see opposite page).

Experimenting with fills

We scanned a sailing ship from *1800 Woodcuts by Thomas Bewick and His School* (Dover, 1962). To simplify the ship and create larger shapes for filling with color, we used Photoshop to remove the crosshatching in the large sails. The edited scan was autotraced in Streamline (**A**) and opened in Illustrator, where we created several variations based on different types of color fills. First we added solid color by selecting the white shapes and filling them with color (**B**). Filling the sails with gradients made them look rounded and a gradient in the background created the illusion of sky blending into ocean (**C**). Illustrator and other PostScript illustration program include ready-made PostScript patterned fills, such as a herringbone pattern, which added a surreal touch to the ship (**D**). (Such patterns can be edited and it's also possible to create your own custom pattern and mask it into a shape.) The ship took on a new look when we added strokes in various colors to the shapes of the sails, ship and waves (**E**). Finally, we scanned an engraving of a lace design by Federic de Vinciolo (Paris, 1606) from *Alphabets and Ornaments* (Dover, 1952). We colored it in Photoshop, saved it as an EPS file, and imported it into Illustrator, where it was masked into the sail shapes, which were grouped as a compound path (**F**).

A
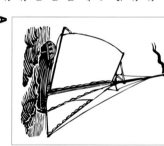

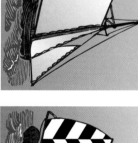

B

C

D

E
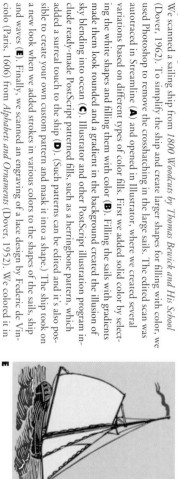

F
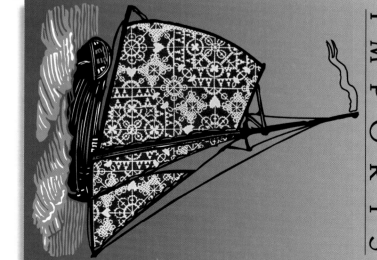

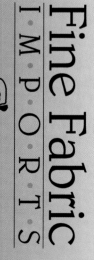

ADDING COLOR TO AN OLD ENGRAVING

When a scanned engraving is saved as a black-and-white (1-bit) TIFF, its white parts will be transparent when imported into CorelDraw, FreeHand or Illustrator. Color can then be added by drawing colored shapes and positioning them behind the scanned image so that they show through the clear areas. This old-fashioned pocket watch was taken from *Goods and Merchandise*, compiled by William Rowe (Dover 1982). The steps we took to transform the line art scan into a cover design are explained at left.

Time Management

50 WAYS TO
INCREASE YOUR
WORKDAY
EFFECIENCY

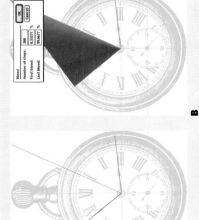

C

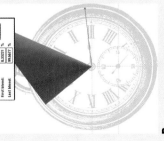

B

ADDING POSTSCRIPT COLOR
We imported our 1-bit clock scan into FreeHand. Then, to create a color gradient we drew a red line from the center to the rim of the dial, cloned it and rotated the clone, turning it green. A third blue line was drawn out to the corner of the image and cloned so that a duplicate line lay directly on top of the original (**A**). Using the Blend function, the selected endpoints of the red and blue line form a radial blend (**B**). The duplicate blue line was brought to the front and blended to the green line to complete the two-stage color sweep (**C**). A similar blend was made on the seconds dial with a blue line and a white line (**D**). Bringing the engraving to the top layer, we drew two arc segments following the rim of the dial (**E**), then hid the engraving layer (**F**). Each of the two blended color sweeps was cut and pasted into the arc segments, trimming the shapes to fit neatly within the watch dial (**G**). The final image (at right) shows the scanned image placed over the color elements.

A

D

E

F

G

FLIPPING, ROTATING AND SKEWING

Playing with scanned shapes can be a good source of new design ideas. Here are a few of our favorite tricks: copying a shape and flipping it to create a symmetrical composition, rotating the same shape to make a mandala-like design or combining skewed copies to make a free-form design or to create cast shadows from silhouettes. Note that when repeated shapes are combined or juxtaposed, the spaces between them becomes important design elements as well.

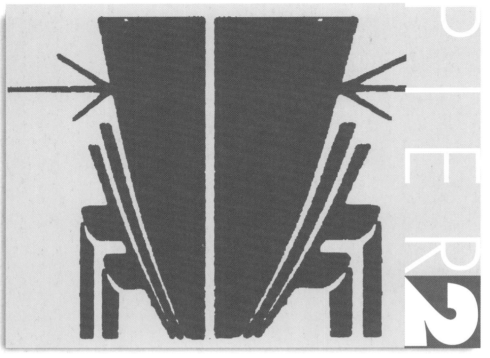

Flipping
Flipping a copy of the ship across the horizontal axis creates the appearance of a reflection in water. The ocean liner icon is taken from *Handbook of Pictorial Symbols* (Dover, 1976).

Rotating
A fish icon scanned from *Visual Elements 1* (Rockport Publishers, 1989) was rotated to create a strong, circular design.

Skewing and rotating
Overlapping layers of repeated, distorted shapes in various sizes and colors adds variety to a simple design idea. Our leaf is from *2001 Decorative Cuts and Ornaments* (Dover, 1988).

Skewing
A skewed clone makes a fine shadow. The line art is from *1,001 Advertising Cuts from the Twenties and Thirties* (Dover, 1987).

FALL SEMESTER

Experimenting

A bird from *Authentic Chinese Cut-Paper Designs* (Dover, 1988) became the basis of several variations of stroke treatment. First the scan was autotraced in Streamline, opened in FreeHand and stroked with a thin white line (**A**). We then increased the weight of the stroke and colored it brown, filling parts of the design with indigo and others with red (**B**). We changed the fill color to green, cloned the entire design and sent the clone to the back. Then we doubled the thickness of the stroke and changed the line color to orange. Finally we sent a second clone to the bottom and quadrupled the stroke width, coloring it pale yellow (**C**).

CHANGING STROKE

The character of simple line art can be dramatically changed by applying strokes of different thicknesses and colors. Just as colored or patterned fills work best on art with simple shapes, ornamental strokes are best applied to drawings made up of simple, clear lines. In a Post-Script illustration program strokes can be applied to paths at any weight (thick or thin), as solid or dashed and in any color. Also, strokes of different weights can be layered on top of each other to produce a banded look.

C

A bold use of outlines and color.
The sun symbol was autotraced after scanning it from *1800 Woodcuts by Thomas Bewick and His School* (Dover, 1962). In FreeHand we filled the face with yellow and stroked it with magenta. Then we filled the rays with green and stroked them with red. Then we filled the remaining elements of the image with black and stroked them with yellow, giving a vibrant effect in keeping with the theme of the graphic.

Got Sunscreen?

A

B

COMBINING SCANNED ELEMENTS

What if you've found the perfect person in a book of clip art, but the background is not quite right. Or the border you like is in another book at another size, in a slightly different style. No problem. By using a combination of bitmap editing, autotracing and PostScript editing, you can combine clip art from different sources to create exactly the image you want. We used various techniques to create a music book cover.

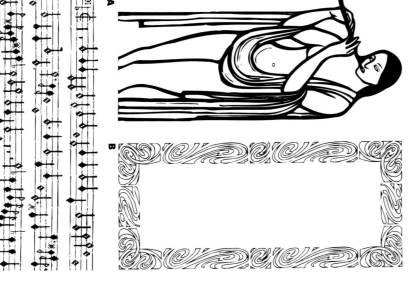

A

B

C

Playing with a cover design

To create a book cover, we started by scanning an *art nouveau*-style bookplate of a woman playing a double flute, taken from *Treasury of Book Ornament and Decoration* (Dover, 1986). We used Photoshop to delete the elaborate decorative border, pear tree, ground elements and one of the flutes. The edited figure was autotraced in Streamline (**A**). We then scanned a more simple border in a similar style from *Decorative Frames and Borders* (Dover, 1973) and rotated it by 90 degrees in Photoshop. This scan was also autotraced in Streamline (**B**). We also scanned a part of a Renaissance music manuscript from *Music: A Pictorial Archive of Woodcuts & Engravings* (Dover, 1980). We used Photoshop to remove the text elements and move the music staves closer together before autotracing with Streamline (**C**).

After autotracing each image-edited element, we opened the three pieces of scanned art in Illustrator for further editing. The border was adapted to fit a wider rectangular format, the music notation was stepped and repeated to create a textured background, the woman was positioned within the frame and type was added (**D**). Color was added to create final full-color art (**E**).

D

E

DESIGNING WITH SCANNED SILHOUETTES

Silhouettes are wonderfully versatile design elements that work well at any scale. What makes a silhouette successful is the way in which it focuses the eye on pure *shape*. Without distracting attributes, such as texture or detail, the power of silhouettes lies in their simplicity.

Negative and positive

We could have placed these silhouettes side by side and made a perfectly reasonable business card. But by superimposing the negative shape of the cat over the positive shape of the dog we have created a much more interesting design. Our pets are from *Old Fashioned Silhouettes* (Dover, 1988).

POCONOS
ANIMAL
CLINIC

1234 Lake Street
Poconos Pines
PA 18352
7O3 456 789O

Q u a c k e r s

Appetizers

Low contrast

The bold shapes of silhouettes remain powerful even when printed in gray on a pale gray stock. Another similarly subtle effect can be obtained by printing the image in varnish. Our silhouette of a painter is also from *Old Fashioned Silhouettes* (Dover, 1988).

Blocks of color

When silhouetted shapes are subdivided into smaller areas by white lines you have an opportunity to introduce several colors into the design. The duck is from *Visual Elements 1* (Rockport Publishers, 1989)

CREATING A BUSINESS IDENTITY

Copyright-free clip art can be a wonderful source of ideas for logo designs and other business graphics, especially when the design budget is limited. We used clip art scanned from a Dover book of music illustrations to create a logo and a complete package of business stationary for a new mail-order musical instrument business. The 19th century engravings were adapted to fit our needs and combined with an appropriate display type to create a logo that is not only attractive and cost-effective, but which visually expresses the "old world" European feeling and values that permeate this particular business venture.

Assembling the raw materials

We started our business identity project by scanning two accordion illustrations from Music: A Pictorial Archive of Woodcuts and Engravings (Dover, 1980). To create a simple graphic for the logo, we used Photoshop to edit the scan of the man playing a concertina (A) and delete all but the right hand and the instrument. We also deleted some of the white elements on the concertina near the hand so that the image would be more clearly readable (B). We then converted the scan to bitmap mode so that its white areas would become transparent when layered over a background (C). We also opened the scan in Illustrator and used it as a guide for creating a background shape (D) that could be placed behind the transparent bitmap (E).

The engraving of a boy playing an accordion was quite dark in the original (F) so we used Photoshop to lighten the whites and midtones (G) and also created a cropped, bitmapped version that could be used for layering. Saving a TIFF in bitmap mode also makes it possible to assign a color to the graphic when it is imported into a color layout or PostScript illustration program. For example, when importing the graphic into the PageMaker layout for this book we were able to assign it a color of muted brick (H).

A

B

C

D

E

F

G

H

Creating a logo and business card

To create a logo we combined the edited concertina graphic with the business name set in Arcadia, a condensed display font from Adobe that perfectly fit the idea of "squeeze." We used Garamond Condensed to set the rest of the type for the business card, which served as a template for the rest of the business graphics

Designing a web graphic

Most businesses have web sites, even if their sales are not conducted over the internet, but for a mail-order company like Squeezeworks.com, a web site is a given. We used the same graphics created for the printed business materials to create a navigation graphic to be placed along the left-hand side of the company's web pages. By using graphically related elements, customers can readily identify the Squeezeworks "look" whether it comes to them online or in the mail. For more information on using scans for web site graphics see Chapter 13, Scanning for the Web.

Putting together basic business stationery package

Using the business card as a starting point, we created designs for a letterhead sheet and #10 envelope, using two colors of ink (black and rust) on a pale purple/gray paper. The contact information was formatted slightly differently on each of the three pieces, to fit the size and needs of each. To provide textural interest for the letterhead sheet we included a pale gray overlay of the concertina man graphic. Also, to distinguish the envelope design, we added a pale gray background behind the logo graphic. We also adapted the letterhead sheet to produce a black-and-white invoice and included a pale gray overlay of the accordion boy.

Overlapping

The two icons for this book cover design are from *Handbook of Pictorial Symbols* (Dover, 1976). When imported into a page layout program the white areas of line art scans that are saved in 1-bit (bitmap) mode are transparent, making it possible to combine them in overlapping designs.

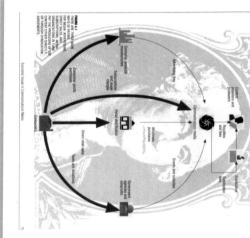

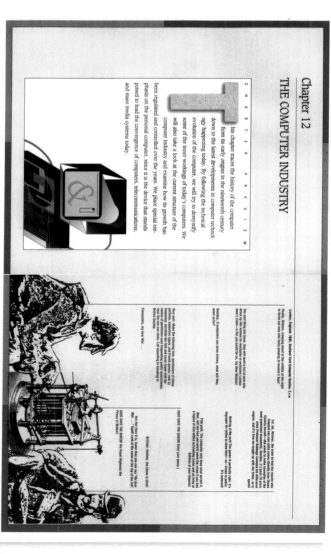

USING SCANNED ART IN A PAGE LAYOUT PROGRAM

Page layout programs make it possible to modify imported scanned art by repeating, enlarging, reducing, cropping, adding color, rotating, flipping and skewing. When integrated with type and other graphic elements, scans can be woven into the fabric of the page and given a new meaning in a context different from that of their original source. Compositions can be elaborate multi-layered montages, or nothing more than a simple crop.

Using line art scans in page layouts

In a page from a college textbook, an enlarged scan of part of a bank note forms a background for a diagram on media financing (**A**). In another spread from the same book, Messrs. Holmes and Watson contemplate a 19th Century computer (**B**).

A

B

6 Applying Artists' Techniques

Working from Photo References

CREATING AND EDITING "PHOTO SCRAP"

Making illustrations from scanned clip art (as we've done in the previous chapter) is fun, fast and cheap. But sometimes we need an original drawing—a technical rendering of a particular object, for example, or an illustration in a modern or unique style. Alas, not all illustrators and designers are good drafters. That's when a camera becomes an indispensable tool for providing reference photographs of objects we want to draw.

ARTISTS AND PHOTO REFERENCES

How do artists translate the three-dimensional world into two-dimensional patterns on paper? In the 1600s Vermeer used a *camera lucida* to project his subjects onto a flat surface for tracing, giving his paintings a photographic quality. Since the invention of photography artists have modified this technique by using photos as references, especially for figures. For example, the early 20th century poster artist Alphonse Mucha used photographs extensively. In *The Artist and the Camera* (Yale University Press, 1999) Jack Rennert writes, "Comparing Mucha's design with the photos from which he worked gives us useful insight into the artistic process. It is clear that no photograph was ever slavishly copied; it represented only a point of departure from which inspiration takes over. With his meticulous attention to detail, Mucha certainly used the pictures to check things such as the precise position of fingers on a hand holding something—often a stumbling block for even otherwise competent artists—as well as for a correct perspective and spatial relations between people and objects. Beyond that, the heart of every design is an expression of the artist's soul." So, the first step in the drawing process for many illustrators is to find or take appropriate photos and to copy their important lines and shapes, either by eye or by tracing.

Using a camera as a drawing aid serves three important purposes: First, it quickly performs the work of converting a three-dimensional scene into a two-dimensional representation with all the correct detail and perspective; second, it produces unique images with content and style that you determine; and third, using your own photos as references means you avoid violating the copyrights of photographers whose work (clipped from old magazines, for example) you may have saved in your files. So it's a good idea to carry some type of camera with you often, to be ready to capture interesting images as they appear. Soon you'll have an impressive collection of personal "photo scrap."

CAPTURING PHOTO REFERENCES

There are three options for creating reference photos.

POLAROID SNAPSHOTS

For immediate help, keep a Polaroid camera handy in the studio. Do you need to know what a right hand looks like when holding a pair of scissors? Photograph your own hand and one minute later you have exactly the

reference you need. The Polaroid print can be traced over by hand or can be scanned.

DIGITAL PHOTOS

Keep a digital camera handy. These new tools combine conventional photography and scanning in one step by recording your images as electronic files rather than on film. (John Odam's *Start with a Digital Camera* [Peachpit, 1999] is an excellent introduction to the use of digital photography in design.) Digital photos can be used as templates for computer tracing or can be printed on paper and then traced by hand.

CONVENTIONAL PHOTOGRAPHY

It's also possible to set up the particular objects and poses you need, photograph them with a 35 mm camera, and take the film to your local one-hour or one-day photo lab and have it output as prints (which you can scan) or as already scanned images on a CD-ROM disk.

EDITING PHOTO REFERENCES

Photographs that will be used as templates or references for drawing do not have to be perfectly composed, or

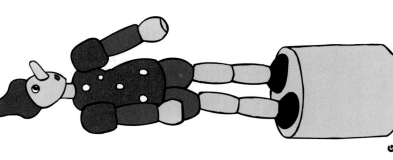

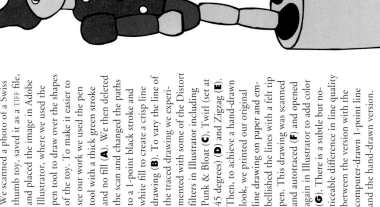

F **E** **D** **C** **B** **A** **G**

properly exposed, or even well-focused. As long as the essentials are there, you can use an image-editing program to edit your scanned photo as necessary—cropping, sharpening, improving contrast—to bring out the detail you need. The goal in this case is to produce an image with clear outlines and edges, so that it's easy to trace. Sometimes it's good to create and print two or more edited versions of an image and trace by hand over each of them to get the best detail in all areas. See page 50 for an example of this and also see Chapter 4, "Editing Scanned Images," starting on page 15.

TRACING IN AN ILLUSTRATION PROGRAM

Once you have a serviceable photo scan, it can be converted to a line drawing in a number of ways. If the object is fairly simple, or contains many straight lines or geometrical shapes, it may be easiest to import the scan into a PostScript illustration program and draw over the outlines and shapes with conventional PostScript drawing tools. Recognizing the traditional importance of photo references for illustration, PostScript drawing programs include the ability to import bitmapped scans as "templates" for tracing. Especially with human-made objects—for example, houses, vehicles, machines, cityscapes and so on—it makes sense to take advantage of the precise drawing tools in a PostScript drawing program. Objects like this often look best when rendered with very clean, smooth lines of uniform width, similar to those produced with a Rapidograph pen. This sort of drawing works especially well for technical or catalog illustrations, which benefit from being clear, uncluttered and easy to recognize.

SOFTENING THE POSTSCRIPT LINE

Suppose you've used a PostScript illustration program to trace over a geometrical subject such as a house and

now you want to soften the look of the crisp, mechanical line work. There are several ways to modify your PostScript lines.

APPLYING POSTSCRIPT FILTERS

Illustrator and FreeHand include a number of filters that make it possible to alter line drawings in interesting ways. These include effects such as roughing, twirling and bloating. They work by moving the PostScript control points in certain ways.

ADDING HANDMADE STROKES

One way to soften the PostScript line is to print a copy of your PostScript drawing on a piece of paper and draw over it by hand with a pen or pencil to make the line more interesting. This altered drawing can then be scanned. You could also open the PostScript line drawing directly in an image-editing program and paint on it to embellish the line. In either case, the edited version can be used as-is, as a bitmapped image, or can be autotraced to return it to PostScript format.

LINE VARIATION IN POSTSCRIPT

It's also possible to import a scan as a template in Illustrator, FreeHand or CorelDraw and draw over it with a "freehand" tool, set to pressure-sensitive mode and used with a tablet and stylus. Changes in pressure on the tablet will cause changes in the thickness of the line.

Tracing on-screen

We scanned a photo of a Swiss thumb toy, saved it as a TIFF file, and placed the image in Adobe Illustrator, where we used the pen tool to draw over the shapes of the toy. To make it easier to see our work we used the pen tool with a thick green stroke and no fill (**A**). We then deleted the scan and changed the paths to a 1-point black stroke and white fill to create a crisp line drawing (**B**). To vary the line of the traced drawing we experimented with some of the Distort filters in Illustrator including Punk & Bloat (**C**), Twirl (set at 45 degrees) (**D**) and Zigzag (**E**). Then, to achieve a hand-drawn look, we printed our original line drawing on paper and embellished the lines with a felt tip pen. This drawing was scanned and autotraced (**F**) and opened again in Illustrator to add color (**G**). There is a subtle but noticeable difference in line quality between the version with the computer-drawn 1-point line and the hand-drawn version.

Which of us could achieve this exactitude…this delicate modeling…indeed, what a wonderful thing photography is—but one dare not say that aloud.
—Jean-Auguste Dominique Ingres, 1780–1867

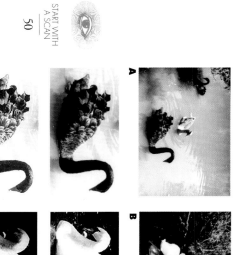

A

B

C

D

E

TRACING BY HAND

The processes of scanning and then tracing in a PostScript illustration program are somewhat antithetical to the values of hand drawing, especially the irregular, warm line produced by actually dragging a pencil across a piece of paper. But by working back and forth between scanning and drawing by hand, it's possible to conserve the special thick-and-thin line quality of traditional artwork, while still taking advantage of the powerful production features of computer graphics—for example, the ability to quickly add smooth color or color gradations and to produce color separations. We have often found it easier, more satisfactory, and more satisfying to use traditional methods of tracing (using pencil on tracing paper or acetate over the photograph) and then to scan the resulting drawing. This is especially true when your scanned photo is of a natural object—such as a face, a human figure, plants or animals.

PRODUCING A THICK-AND-THIN LINE DRAWING

There are several ways to create a warm, thick-and-thin line quality in electronic art that is based on a photo reference.

DRAWING BY HAND

The most straightforward way is to actually use your hand. Print an enlarged copy of your reference scan and draw over it with a pencil or a pen, using a light table and tracing paper or acetate. Scan the hand-drawing and either use the scan as final art or convert it to PostScript by autotracing it in Outline mode, which will convert the line strokes into shapes that retain the line quality of the original.

LINE VARIATION IN A PAINT PROGRAM

Another way to duplicate the drawn-by-hand look is to open the reference scan in a program like Photoshop or Painter, assign it to a nonactive layer, and use a digitizing tablet and stylus to draw over it in an active layer. Painter contains many drawing tools—such as pencils, pastels and watercolor brushes— that duplicate natural media very convincingly.

Editing and tracing photo references

To demonstrate the importance of editing photos that will be used as templates, we started with two photos of swans—a black one with dark midtones (**A**), and a white one with light midtones (**B**). We converted each scan to grayscale and then lightened the midtones in the black swan and sharpened it using Unsharp Mask to exaggerate the edges. This made it easier to see the details of the feathers (**C**). Conversely, we darkened the midtones in the white swan to bring out more feather detail and also applied Unsharp Mask (**D**). We then printed these edited scans and traced over the shapes with pencil on matte acetate to produce hand drawings of the black and white swans (**E**). The two drawings were autotraced and combined in Illustrator to produce a book cover (**F**).

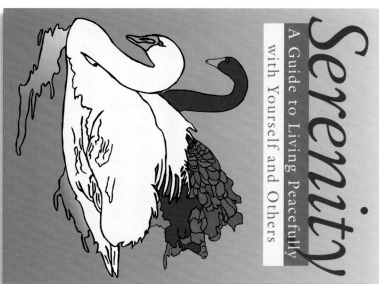

F

Serenity
A Guide to Living Peacefully with Yourself and Others

REFINING THE HAND-DRAWN LINE

Suppose you've used a pencil or pen to produce a drawing by tracing over a scanned photo, but now you want the drawing to look cleaner and more hard-edged. You can tighten up the look of your hand drawing by scanning it and then autotracing the scan in Streamline's Centerline mode, which produces a series of PostScript paths which can be assigned a uniform line width. This technique can be used with any line drawings, whether based on photo scans or not.

Making a centerline autotracing

To create line drawings of a sunflower, we started with a scan of a color photo taken by Florence Ashford (**A**), converted it to grayscale and boosted the contrast and focus to create a clear version for hand-tracing (**B**). We printed a laser copy of the image, enlarged so that it filled a letter-size sheet, and traced over the important shapes with pencil on matte acetate. We went over the pencil lines with a black felt tip marker, then scanned the ink drawing and saved it as a TIFF (**C**).

Autotracing in Streamline made it possible to produce several different versions of the drawing, based on the same scanned pencil sketch. First, we did a Centerline autotrace, with the Separate Shapes option checked. This converted the drawing into a pattern of contiguous shapes. We opened the autotracing in Illustrator, and specified that all the paths have a .5-point black stroke and a white fill. This produced a smooth, simple line drawing (**D**). Next, we filled each of the shapes with a solid color, sampled from the original photo (see Quick Tip) (**E**). As a variation, we removed the black stroke from the shapes, which produced a look similar to a silkscreen print (**F**). We also tried filling each shape with a gradient (**G**).

A

B

C

D

E

F

G

QUICK TIP

To quickly add color to shapes autotraced from a scanned photograph, import the photograph into the Illustrator file containing the line drawing and click on color areas with the eyedropper tool to sample colors from the scan. These can be used to fill the shapes you have selected.

PAINTING ELECTRONICALLY

Another way of using a scanned hand-drawing is to create an electronically painted illustration. We used Corel Painter to add color and special effects to a scanned pencil drawing of apples, which we had made by tracing over a black-and-white version of the photo using pencil on a sheet of matte acetate. Painter provides a vast store of painting and drawing tools that imitate the look of traditional media, including chalk, felt tip pens, crayons, watercolors, airbrushes, pencils, pen and ink, calligraphy pens, charcoal, oil paints, erasers and liquid, all of which can be customized with regard to size, angle, texture and other features. Working with a digitizing tablet and stylus made it possible to work in a familiar, intuitive way to create illustrations that look convincingly "nondigital." We also experimented with some of Painter's smearing and cloning tools to add special effects to the original apple photo on which our drawing was based.

A

B

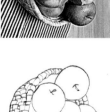

C

Creating a sketch
We scanned a color print of apples (**A**), converted the scan to grayscale and used Unsharp Mask to exaggerate the edges (**B**). Then we printed the grayscale image on paper and drew over it with pen on a piece of tracing paper. The resulting hand drawing was scanned (**C**).

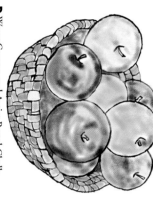

D Waxy Crayon and Artist Pastel Chalk

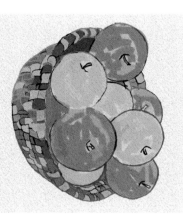

E Broad Water brush over solid color areas

F Impressionist brush with autoclone

Adding color in Painter
We opened our apple sketch in Painter and used a variety of tools to add color. Some brushes, such as the Waxy Crayon, picked up color from the black lines of our original drawing. We used Waxy Crayon on the apples and the Artist Pastel Chalk brush on the basket (**D**). Other tools, such as the Broad Water brush, did not smudge the black line work of the original scan. We placed watercolor strokes over solid color areas created with the Paint Bucket tool and then applied a Hand Made Paper texture (**E**). Painter's autocloning tools make it possible to automatically apply painterly strokes to an image. We use autoclone to apply the Impressionist brush to our original apples photograph, specifying that the brush pick up its colors from the photo (**F**).

G Smear brush

Using Smear to manipulate a photo
We used the Smear brush to stroke through a copy of the original photo, producing an effect similar to that in which artists use tools to manipulate and smear the wet emulsion of a fresh Polaroid print (**G**).

Line Quality, Mood and Montage

ENLARGING SMALL IMAGES FOR SPECIAL EFFECTS

Not everything in life is smooth, clean and perfect—especially on close inspection. Printed images contain rough edges, missing parts, dots, grain, smears and smudges, which when enlarged can assume a rugged grandeur that leads to powerful designs. Extreme enlargement simplifies and abstracts the shapes. The effect can be bold and strong, or playful and funky. Increasing the contrast of an image often accentuates the roughness.

Finding the right candidate for enlargement is sometimes difficult because you can't always anticipate how interesting an image will be when blown up. Since your originals in this case are often small—and tend to be the kind of ephemeral things we throw away—a good place to start looking for small images to scan is the trash. Anything that has irregularity has good potential: rubber stamps, postmarks, cartons, dot-matrix prints, woodcuts, engravings, poor-quality photocopies, faxes and grainy photographs.

Ten times larger than life
A detail of an old package from grandma's sewing box assumes the quality of modern art when enlarged.

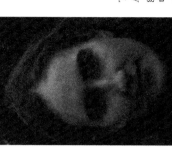

Film grain
An underexposed, grainy photograph, when enlarged on the scanner, can take on the appearance of a painting by Seurat.

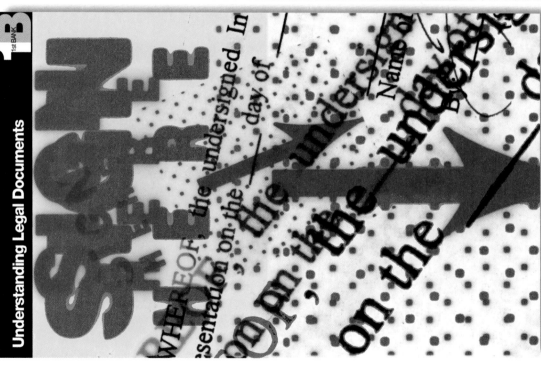

Layering enlarged images
A "sign here" sticker serves as a starting point for a design that accentuates the irregularities in the printing. Here, details of the same image have been overlapped at different scales and angles. Layering plays shape against shape, creating new patterns.

IRREGULAR LINE FROM SMALL INK DRAWINGS

Those calls to technical support that are on interminable hold, or meetings when one's mind wanders can inspire tiny and wonderfully demented pen drawings—usually on blue-lined yellow paper. We like to keep a collection of these doodles because their spontaneous quality sometimes perfectly fits the mood of a design.

When casual pen strokes are enlarged their rhythm becomes broader and more elegant. The smaller the original, the less chance the hand has to fuss with the line, and the less chance the inner art critic will notice what you are drawing.

A yellow background and blue lines (**A**), present problems in the original. In Photoshop we used the Curves controls to eliminate the blue lines and turn the background white (**B**). Overlapping stray doodles were herded up and eliminated with lasso and eraser. Adding color areas to the drawing in broad shapes behind the line work completed the task of transforming a doodle of a menacing-looking car into an illustration (**C**).

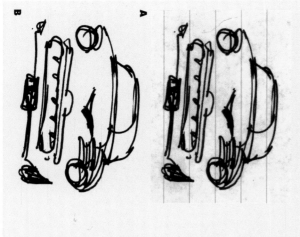

A

B

C

BLENDING LINE ART AND SCANS IN LAYERS

Although much usable public domain art consists of antiquated line art, this does not necessarily limit one's scope in tone, color and texture. Photoshop's powerful layering capability makes it possible to combine many overlays of line art in conjunction with photographic material. The ways in which these layers can interact are almost limitless. Once the composition is established, be daring and experiment with different blending modes such as Lighten, Darken and Difference.

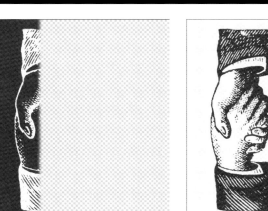

Looking at layers

Examining each layer in Photoshop shows how the elements in our illustration were arranged. The hand-shake drawing on layer 2 was duplicated in layer 3 and inverted and cropped.

Layer 3
75% opacity
Lighten

Layer 2
75% opacity
Overlay

Layer 1
Normal

CREATING A RECURSIVE MONTAGE

Taking one image and repeating it at several different sizes in different layers sometimes makes a montage as rich and interesting as if many images had been used. When you add to this the effect of overlapping colors, the possibilities become almost unlimited. On this page we have used Photoshop's channels and layers to combine three overlapped repeats of the original image.

Swiching channels

Transforming just two of the three primary color channels produces dramatic secondary shapes and unexpected colors. We began by saving the line art scan to RGB color. We scaled down the image in the green channel and inverted it (turned it to negative). We reduced the size of the image in the blue channel slightly and flipped it horizontally. The horses are from *Old Fashioned Silhouettes* (Dover 1988).

Switching monochrome layers

In this example a grayscale scan of an engraving has been placed on three duplicated layers at different scales. One layer has been inverted and another flipped horizontally. The gray tones are made by making some layers semitransparent. Image from *Music: A Pictorial Archive of Woodcuts & Engravings* (Dover 1980).

7 | Creating Textures and Backgrounds

Textures from Print and Paper

MONOCHROME AND COLOR TEXTURES

Unlike patterns that have repeating elements, *textures* are random areas of irregular tone and color such as those in textured or handmade papers. In this section we illustrate the use of textures derived from paper and printed materials. In the next section (page 66), we show how to create and use textures derived from cloth, scanned objects and photos.

Textures are useful in page layout as a substitute for tint boxes or areas of flat color. They can create the fascinating illusion of a different kind of paper on part of the page. When textures are used behind type they should be subtle and unobtrusive. It's important that a textured background not interfere with the legibility of the type placed over it.

Textures can also be used as elements in digital illustration to enrich and humanize the mechanical appearance that often appears in computer-generated graphics. In bitmapped images, textures can be blended or painted into different areas of a composition. In PostScript art, textures can be placed as TIFF files behind solid shapes or pasted into different areas in the illustration.

Textures also play an important role in multimedia, slide presentations and on-line graphics, by setting off photographs and lettering. As with print media, be careful to maintain the legibility of any type placed over scanned textures.

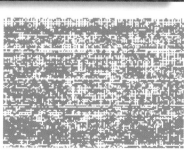

Colleqe Writing Skills 4th Edition
Peder Jones and Jay Furness

Using clip art textures
Four textures were scanned from *Background Patterns, Textures and Tints* (Dover, 1976). One (bottom left) has been used as a background element in the book cover above. The line art scan was colored in a PostScript drawing program and layered over an area filled with a color.

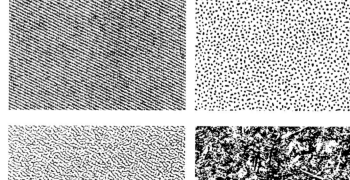

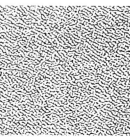

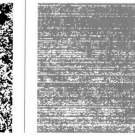

Finding textures in untextured paper
Vellum (left) and plain white bond (right) have no discernible texture, but increasing the contrast of scans of these papers produces rich textures that are actually artifacts of the scanning process.

Look beneath the surface; let not the several quality of a thing nor its worth escape thee.
—Marcus Aurelius Antoninus (121–180 A.D), *Meditations*

SCANNING TEXTURED PAPER

Designers often receive samples from paper companies. In addition to being useful for specifying paper for print jobs, these samples are a wonderful resource for scanned backgrounds. You may also find a selection of papers to purchase and scan at your local art supply store.

Textured papers may have either a surface texture, such as that of watercolor paper or canvas, or may contain embedded particles of various kinds, such as fibers or flecks.

Watercolor

PAPER WITH SURFACE TEXTURE

Paper surface textures are often subtle so it is usually necessary to increase the contrast of the scan to bring out the detail. Papers can be scanned in grayscale mode and tinted with color later. Scans of textured paper may also be amplified or enhanced by applying filter effects—for example, to add noise or to emboss.

Bringing out subtle textures
These textured papers were scanned in grayscale. The contrast was increased 75% and the brightness decreased 5% using Photoshop's Brightness and Contrast controls.

Canvas

Adding color
Color was added to the grayscale charcoal paper scan (**A**) by importing it into a page layout program, selecting it and specifying a color from the color menu (**B**).

A   **B**

Charcoal

Applying paper texture to a handbook cover
Scanned paper was used as a background in this design, making the panel bearing the main graphic stand out.

PAPER WITH EMBEDDED TEXTURE

Flecks of fiber, wood chips and other additives make handmade and specialty papers ideal for use as textured backgrounds. When scanning embedded-texture paper we use a lower contrast setting than for paper with surface texture. The variation in tone should be minimal so that type placed over the background will be readable. The examples shown here include recycled paper, industrial chipboard, marbled parchment, handmade paper and paper made with flower petals.

Permalin Petal (Pink Medley)

Permalin Petal (Desert Bloom)

Sihl Fiber

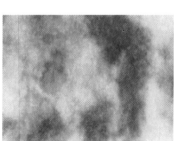

Sihl Parchment

French Paper Packing Carton

French Paper Speckletone

Fox River Confetti (Kaleidoscope)

Fox River Confetti (Yellow)

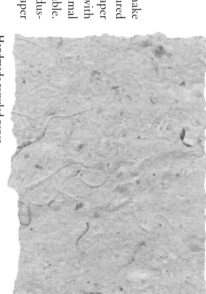

Handmade recycled paper

PAPER SCULPTURE EFFECT WITH CURVATURE AND DROP SHADOWS

By scanning textured paper it´s possible to produce an almost unlimited supply of digital "paper" for virtual paper sculpture.

We began by scanning an elephant icon from *Visual Elements 1* (Rockport Publishers, 1989) (**A**). We used the lasso tool to copy the head and body into separate layers in Photoshop (**B**) and pasted a previously scanned paper texture from another document into each selected body part (**C**).

A

B

C

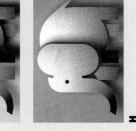
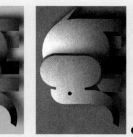

G

H

E

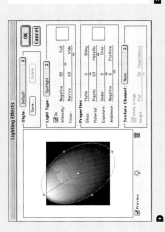

F

D

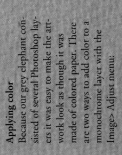

Next we converted the gray-scale file to RGB and applied the lighting effects filter (**D**) to each of the elephant's body part layers to give the appearance of curvature to the simulated paper sculpture shapes (**E**).

The three-dimensional illusion was completed by adding a drop shadow effect to each layer (**F**).

Applying color
Because our grey elephant consisted of several Photoshop layers it was easy to make the artwork look as though it was made of colored paper. There are two ways to add color to a monochrome layer with the Image>Adjust menu:

Hue/Saturation (G)
With the Colorize button checked, the hue slider determines the color and the saturation slider its intensity.

Color Balance (H)
Moving the three sliders away from their centers produces many different color variations that can be applied successively to highlights, midtones and shadows, giving subtle variations in color to the "paper" shapes.

SCANNING HAND-MADE TEXTURES

In this clean computer age it's often a welcome change to get your hands messy with ink, paint and chalk. By using some traditional elementary school techniques it's possible to bring out usable textures from surfaces that do not give good results when scanned directly. Some techniques worth trying include: dabbing paint with a kitchen sponge; using a grease pencil to make rubbings of textured paper, wood or other grainy or raised surfaces; and printing from painted fingers or sliced vegetables. All the examples shown on this page are line art scans of handmade textures.

Using a hand-generated texture in an architecural graphic

The sponge texture on this page was added to the tree shapes to suggest foliage.

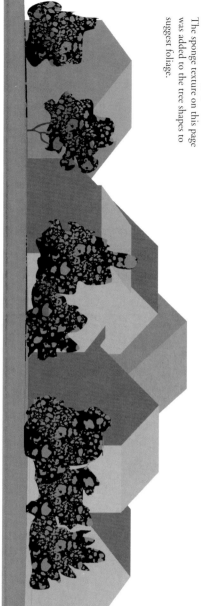

Sponge print

Sponge wipe

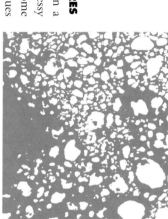

Dry sponge

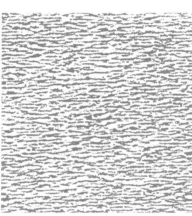

Grease pencil, watercolor paper

Grease pencil, wood

Grease pencil, place mat

Finger print

"PAINTING" WITH SCANNED PENCIL TEXTURES

Repetitive tasks are often done extraordinarily well by a computer. For example, filling in pencil shading between guidelines in a drawing is usually a dull task when done by hand; perhaps enjoyable only as a form of meditation. But by using a scanned pencil texture it's possible to shade in large areas of a drawing almost instantly and always have the privilege of changing your mind. Since both the outline drawing and the swatch of shading are lively marks of your own hand, captured faithfully by the scanner, the resultant drawing does not look mechanical.

If you keep your master drawing as a separate file, several differing variants can be made with alternative shading schemes. Although the example shown here is monochrome, the same basic technique works for color as well.

Shading the truth

Our original drawing was made with a No. 2 pencil on vellum. It was scanned at 300 dpi in grayscale mode and edited so that the background dropped away to white (**A**).

A small patch of pencil shading at medium density (**B**) was copied once, darkened 50% (**C**), copied again and lightened 50% (**D**), using Photoshop's Contrast and Brightness controls.

With all three shading files and the scanned pencil sketch open at the same time, areas of the drawing were selected one by one and filled with texture from each of the shading files.

The method for Photoshop is as follows: first use the magic wand tool to select an area of the drawing that is enclosed by a line. (Adjust the tolerance of the tool if necessary and fix any leaks in the line with the pencil tool.) Make a pencil texture file active and, with the rubber stamp tool, Option/Alt-click inside the window. Now return to the drawing file and paint in the texture with the rubber stamp tool. Only the selected area will receive the texture, keeping it within the boundaries of the line.

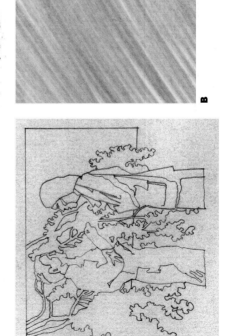

A

B

C

D

WORKING WITH DECORATED PAPER

Decorated paper has long been used in bookbinding and other arts and crafts such as collage, paper sculpture and paper folding. Marbled paper is one of the most common types of decorated paper (see "The Art of Marbling" on the opposite page). Other decorative processes include sponging, spattering, stamping, paste paper, Suminagashi marbling, dyed paper and so on.

Scans of decorated paper can be used as background textures and other design elements for printed pieces as well as for the web. Decorated papers are available from paper supply houses and art supply stores. Some decorative paper is also available as clip art, either in printed form or on CD-ROM. In addition, art supply stores sell paper marbling kits and other supplies that can be used to create your own decorated paper.

Modifying scanned paper

To create decorative elements for an artist's accordion book Janet scanned a piece of hand-made paste paper, selected different parts of the scan and then used Hue/Saturation in Photoshop to change the hue. To "burn" a series of words into the paper she used the type tool to create type outlines and then used Levels to darken the midtones in the type selection areas. For more examples of artist's books see pages 120-121.

Traditional Western marbling with acrylic paints floated on a gelatinous medium

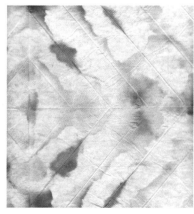

Orizomegami, a Japanese method of folding and dying paper with ink

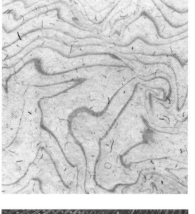

Suminogashi, a Japanese method of floating inks on water

Paste paper, a technique in which flour paste colored with paint is raked with various tools

SOURCES OF DECORATED PAPER

COPYRIGHT-FREE PRINTS OF MARBLED PAPER

Marbleized Paper Patterns in Full Color
by Lauren Clark
Dover Publications
11 East 2nd Street
Mineola, NY 11501

INTERNET SOURCES

www.paperpage.com
Handmade papers

www.artstoreplus.com
A variety of artist papers

www.fascinating-folds.com
Origami and artisan papers

DO-IT-YOURSELF

For instructions on sponging, spattering, paste paper, paper dyeing, marbling and other paper decorating techniques see:
Creative Paper Art: Techniques for Transforming the Surface by Nancy Welch
Sterling Publishing Co.
New York, 1999

ELECTRONIC MARBLING

The traditional paper marbling process begins with the creation of a "stone" pattern made by dropping ink onto a prepared gelatinous surface. The blobs of ink or paint are sometimes used as the final pattern, but more often the colors are "raked" with various combed tools to produce the characteristically delicate swirls of a marbled pattern.

To duplicate a stone pattern electronically, we scanned a handful of buttons, which were placed directly on the scanner. This produced an image containing evenly distributed areas of color. It's also possible to use a photograph as a started point for marbling, so we used a photo of flowers. (If necessary, sections of a photo can be copied, pasted and re-positioned around the image to evenly distribute the color areas, since the objects in the photo will be rendered unrecognizable by the marbling process.) We applied electronic marbling effects to our two scans, using both Photoshop and Painter.

The marbling produced by electronic means looks remarkably similar to hand-marbled designs and can be used for the same sorts of projects—for example, gift wrap, decorative boxes, lamp shades, journal covers, package designs, or backgrounds in book design. For more ideas see Chapter 12, Using Scans in Arts and Crafts, starting on page 117.

Marbling in Photoshop

Traditional marbling starts with a "stone" pattern of ink drops, like this one from *Marbleized Paper Patterns in Full Color* by Lauren Clark (Dover, 1992) (**A**). Our stone patterns consist of scans of buttons and flowers (**B, C**). To electronically marble these images in Photoshop, we first applied the Motion Blur filter to smear the edges of the color in each image (**D, E**) and then applied the Ripple filter to marble it (**F, G**). The marbled flower image (**G**) is shown in detail.

Marbling in Painter

We also opened the blurred version of each scan in Painter and chose the Apply Marbling function, experimenting with the values for spacing, offset, waviness, wavelength and phase, which duplicate the attributes of a marbling rake (**H, I**). For more examples of Painter's effects see "Painting Electronically" on page 52.

see Chapter 12, Using Scans in Arts and Crafts, starting on page 117.

THE ART OF MARBLING

The art of decorating paper with marbled patterns of paint or ink began in ancient Japan, was refined in India, Persia and Turkey, and reached its peak in Europe from the 15th through 17th Centuries. The craft was kept secret by the trade guilds until the first book on marbling, *The Art of Marbling* by Charles Woolnough, was published in England in 1853.

In the traditional technique, pigments are floated on a "size," a gel-like medium made by mixing water with a thickener called Irish Moss, a powdered seaweed. When paint or inks are dropped onto this surface, the rounded drops float and spread, but do not bleed into each other; so it's possible to create patterns of clear color that mimic the beautifully random natural patterns of veined and marbled stone. When these initial "stone" patterns are "raked" by pulling a stylus or comblike row of sharp pins lightly across the surface, the blobs of color are swirled into delicate patterns that resemble those of unfolding ferns or ice filigree on windows. These patterns became extremely popular as decorative papers for bookbinding during the Renaissance, and most of our early examples of marbling are from that source. In fact, the edges of books of financial records were often marbled as a security device, since the removal of any pages would be immediately apparent as a gap in the marbled pattern.

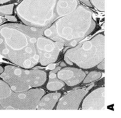

A

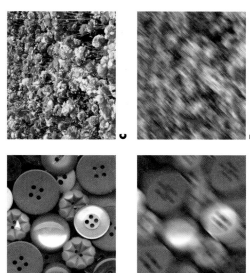

B

C

D

E

F

G

H

I

Textures All Around Us

SCANNING CLOTH

Sources of texture and design for both background and foreground elements abound in the environment around us. Cloth provides an especially rich source of texture and pattern for use in illustration and design. Try scanning your own clothing or rummage through the remnant pile at your local fabric store for small pieces and scraps (and don't forget ribbons and trims). Anything made out of cloth or woven fabric which is fairly flat—for example, hats, belts, purses, scarves and mufflers, place mats, napkins, tablecloths, sheets and pillowcases, upholstery and so on—can be scanned and used in a design. Garage or estate sales are a good place to look for fabric that has been worked by hand with embroidery, crochet, tatting and so forth. Import stores are good sources of handmade cloth, clothing, and accessories.

TYPES OF CLOTH

WOVEN CLOTH

Some cloth has its characteristic look because of the way it's woven. For example, satin is very tightly woven to produce a smooth, shiny surface, while burlap is so coarse you can see the spaces between the threads. Fabrics with a distinctive weave are usually monochromatic and because of their subtle coloring and texture are most often used for clothing that is tailored or elaborately sewn, in which the structure of the garment is the "subject" while the fabric functions as a background. In the same way, these types of fabrics make excellent scanned backgrounds for use in design. They can also be used to provide a texture for a scanned photo (see page 68).

PRINTED CLOTH

By contrast, with printed cloth, the simple woven fabric is the background and the printed design is the

PRINTED CLOTH

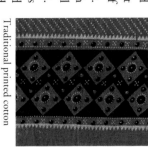

Traditional printed cotton from India

MULTICOLORED WOVEN CLOTH

Hand-loomed weaving of yarn and dyed wool, United States

ORNAMENTED CLOTH

Embroidered table napkin from China

CUT AND STITCHED CLOTH

Cut and stitched "mola" from Central America

Traditional printed floral pattern on wool challis scarf from Russia

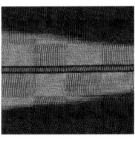

Printed table cloth from the United States, 1940s

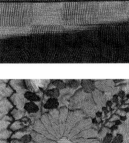

Woven silk from an antique Japanese kimono

KNITTED AND CROCHETED FABRIC

Embroidered dress from Mexico

Hand-stitched and appliquéd purse from Thailand

Woven belt from Central America

Machine-crocheted sweater from the United States

Fair Isles-style sweater hand-knitted in the United States

subject. Hence, scans of printed cloth can work as textured backgrounds only if they are very monochromatic or if they are screened back by lightening and decreasing contrast.

Designs printed on cloth are copyrighted just as any other commercially used designs are, so take care when scanning them for design use. It's safest either to use antique fabrics or patterns that are very generic or traditional, such as the small flowers of calico or the checks of gingham.

OTHER TYPES OF ORNAMENTED CLOTH

There are many ways of ornamenting simple dyed or printed cloth. Plain cloth can be decorated by sewing on it (cross-stitch or embroidery), by cutting, folding and stitching it into patterns (appliqué), or by cutting and sewing small pieces into a quilt. Ornamented cloth often has such strong design qualities that it does not work well as a background, but it can be very effective when used in borders, as spot art or as a focal point for a poster, brochure or announcement.

EDITING SCANNED CLOTH

Scanned cloth can be edited in an image-editing program such as Photoshop in order to produce a variety of effects. For example, it can be filtered to produce a patterned design, it can be lightened or darkened, elements of it can be selected to be used as spot art, and elements can be stepped-and-repeated to create a patterned background. Elements from scanned cloth can also be saved as "tiles" for use in generating backgrounds for Web sites (see pages 74 and 132).

Scanning and altering cloth

We scanned a variety of different types of cloth (opposite page) and used Photoshop to vary various hue, apply various filters, and silhouette or repeat elements. The filters used were those included with Photoshop. The filter family and filter name are given for each.

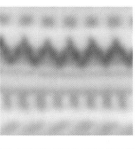

Design element silhouetted

Stylize, Find Edges filter applied; color inverted

Midtones lightened with Levels; blurred with Gaussian Blur

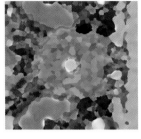

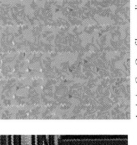

Flowers selected and repeated; one flower element selected, hue changed, and repeated

Artistic, Palette Knife filter applied

Artistic, Cut Out filter applied

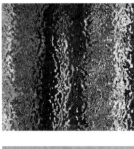

Distort, Ocean Ripple filter applied

Brush strokes, Sumi-e filter applied; lightened with Levels

Square area selected, copied and rotated

Sketch, Chalk and Charcoal filter applied; Color added and adjusted with Hue/Saturation

Color inverted

Flower element selected to create a vignette; drop shadow added

A

B

C

Texturing photos with cloth
To add a soft texture to a scanned still life of pears (**A**), we scanned a piece of worn denim from an old pair of jeans and increased the contrast (**B**). We opened the still life scan in Photoshop and pasted the denim scan into a separate layer above that of the photo image. We then blended the denim with the still life using Overlay mode at 60% opacity (**C**).

Scanned cloth can also be used as a custom paper texture in Painter and can be imported for use in Photoshop's Texturizer filter.

USING CLOTH AS AN IMAGE TEXTURE

Scanned cloth works especially well as a "paper" texture, which will show through any images that are painted over it as though it were a real textured surface. This effect can be achieve in Photoshop by combining a scanned photo with a scanned cloth texture using the blending modes and transparency controls.

USING SCANNED FABRICS IN DESIGN

Scanned fabrics can be used effectively in graphic design by fitting the cloth to the original feeling and origins of the design use. For example, fabrics such as traditional watered silk or brocade tend to be woven in subdued colors and convey a sense of wealth and refinement. Scans of these fabrics can work well as backgrounds for designs associated with upscale events or products, such as a charity fashion show or a fine soap label. On the other hand, cloth that is brightly colored, with bold, somewhat primitive, repetitive and lively motifs looks handsome when used as a border or as a form of spot art for uses that require and can handle strong graphics, such as concert posters, album or book covers, or note cards.

A fabric collage illustration
We scanned fabrics from India and used areas of each to create a collage. The original striped fabric was used to create a sky. To make the ground we copied and rotated the striped fabric and edited the colors, using Hue/Saturation to shift the blue to brown and Selective Color to change the pink to yellow. We also used Hue/Saturation to vary the color in the striped square behind the initial E. The other fabric was used to fill the outline of an elephant silhouette scanned from *Old-Fashioned Silhouettes* (Dover, 1988) and also to fill the E, which is an edited Benguiat character.

E is for elephant

SCANNING OBJECTS

We've seen that interesting textures occur in the flat patterns of paper and cloth, but small three-dimensional objects can also be scanned and used as textures, either alone (as with a large fern leaf) or in groups (as with a collection of seashells). One of the reasons we like to see and use textures in design is that they provide a warm, varied surface that can soften the edges of a design. This may be related to our human visual experience of the natural world around us, which is covered over with subtle textures created by variations in surface structure and light conditions. The glass of a flatbed scanner is a perfect place for assembling groups of small objects, both natural and human-made, that can become subtle, satisfying textures.

MECHANICS OF SCANNING OBJECTS

Choose objects that are small, not too heavy and relatively clean—that is, not wet or crumbly. Pebbles, small bits of wood, seashells, food items, jewelry and plant materials work well. Small manufactured objects such as paper clips, screws, marbles, rubber bands, and baskets can also provide the variation of surface and light that is so attractive to our eyes. Some artists have even scanned slowly while small animals—such as a pet frog or snake—slithered across the scanner glass at will, creating interesting patterns of movement. (For more ideas see the object scans on the next two pages and "Art at Your Finger Tips" on page 109.)

It takes time to arrange small objects on the scanner so that their shapes interlock or overlap to produce a texture without gaps, if this is the effect you want. Or you may want to deliberately include a gap that will later provide a space for type. The process of arranging objects on the scanner is similar to that of the photographer or painter arranging materials for a still life.

A
If the objects you've chosen are very thick, remove the scanner lid so that it's not in the way. Place a large piece of paper, foam core board or a box lid over the objects to serve as a background in place of the inner surface of the lid. Some objects, such as marbles, will roll around on the scanner glass. Contain your more mobile arrangements by surrounding them with metal rulers or small books or whatever is handy. Arrange things so that the props can be cropped out of the final image without affecting the final desired size of the scan.

EDITING SCANNED TEXTURES

If a texture scan will be used as an illustration—for example, as a photographic border—then improve the contrast and sharpness as you would for a scanned photo. If the texture will be used as a background, and especially if type will appear directly over it, reduce the contrast, lighten the tonal range and apply a soft blur.

Scanning one object or many

Scans of objects can produce both crisp images that illustrate content or soft backgrounds that create a mood. For a menu we started with a scan of a fern and edited it in Photoshop to create a lightened panel which could serve as a background for text (**A**). For a book cover design we scanned a group of seashells, opened the scan in Photoshop and created a gradient in a masking channel so that we could apply editing effects in a graduated way from top to bottom. We edited the hue so that the shells became blue-toned and also darkened the midtones, with the mask ensuring that most of the changes appeared toward the bottom of the scan. We also lightened a strip of the scan behind the type (**B**).

B

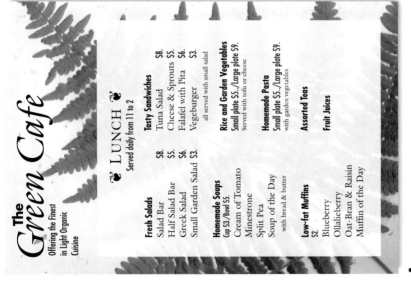

USING FILTERS ON SCANNED OBJECTS

Scans of textural objects can be used as design elements in many ways. At full color saturation they can be used as decorative borders or bars, or they can be lightened to serve as backgrounds for type or other elements. In both cases, the original objects will be recognizable. But sometimes a scan of a handful of colored pasta or bright game pieces, for example, works to provide a quick way to capture masses of color and pattern for use as a starting point for applying the various filters that are native to Photoshop, as well as those made by third parties. Filters can be used to mask the identity of the objects in the scan (producing pleasingly textured decorative patterns that make them suitable for use as backgrounds) or can also be used to make textured objects more stylized or accentuated so that their forms are highlighted in an interesting way. These two pages show some of the variety of objects that can be scanned as textures, along with a filtered version of each scan.

Filtering scanned objects

Simple objects, often readily available around the house, garden and office, can be placed directly on the scanner and used as textures or as starting points for further editing and filtering. The filters used here are those included with Photoshop. The filter family and filter name are given for each.

TEXTURES ALL AROUND US

The world is full of objects that can be scanned and used as textures. Examples include:

Baskets

Food items (vegetables, fruits, pasta, beans)

Fur and leather

Hardware (nails, screws, tacks)

Jewelry and beads

Marbles

Office supplies (paper clips, rubber bands)

Paper and packing materials

Plant materials (leaves, sticks, flowers)

Rocks, pebbles, gems

Sea shells

Toys and game pieces

For a longer list of objects and artifacts to scan see "Art at Your Fingertips" on page 109.

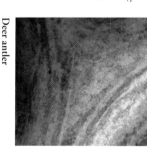

Deer antler

Distort, Ripple

Dry beans

Blur, Motion Blur

Tin can

Stylize, Find Edges

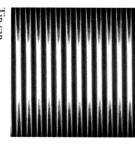

Candles

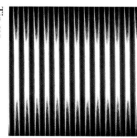

Render, Difference Clouds

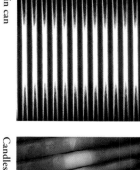

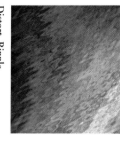

Paper clips

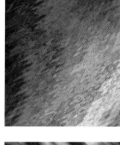

Distort, Ripple

Dried corn

Plastic combs

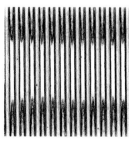

Feather

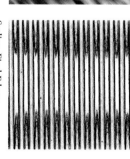

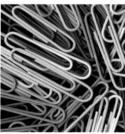

Texture, Patchwork

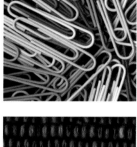

Brush Strokes, Sprayed Strokes

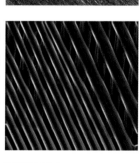

Stylize, Glowing Edges

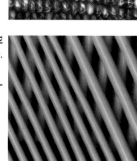

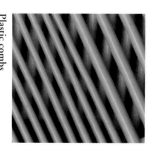

Distort, Shear

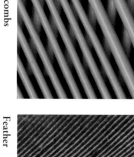

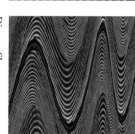

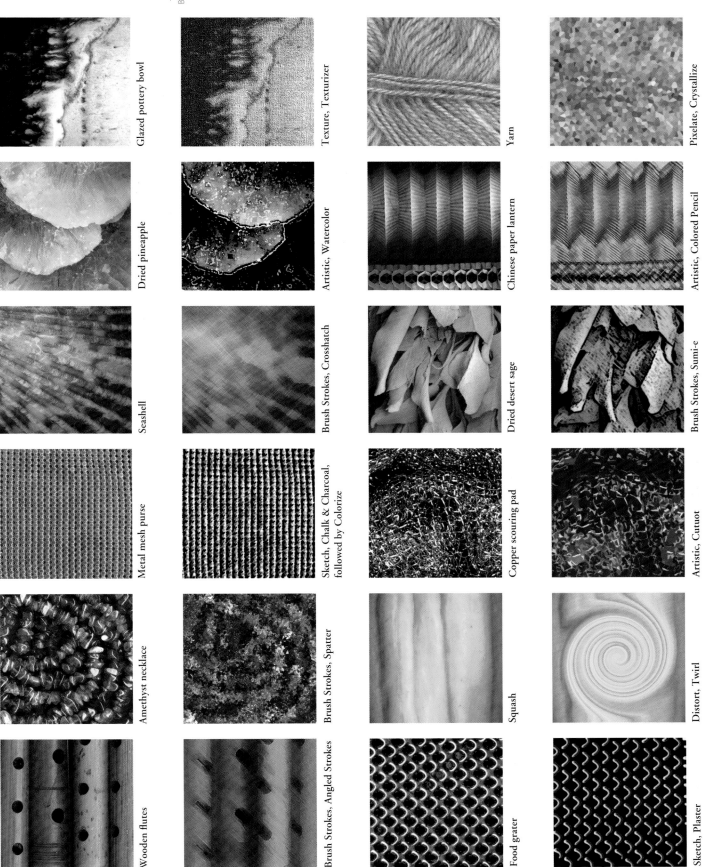

Glazed pottery bowl

Texture, Texturizer

Yarn

Pixelate, Crystallize

Dried pineapple

Artistic, Watercolor

Chinese paper lantern

Artistic, Colored Pencil

Seashell

Brush Strokes, Crosshatch

Dried desert sage

Brush Strokes, Sumi-e

Metal mesh purse

Sketch, Chalk & Charcoal, followed by Colorize

Copper scouring pad

Artistic, Cutuot

Amethyst necklace

Brush Strokes, Spatter

Squash

Distort, Twirl

Wooden flutes

Brush Strokes, Angled Strokes

Food grater

Sketch, Plaster

USING PHOTOS AS TEXTURES

Whether it's urban, suburban or rural, our everyday environment is awash with texture. A trip around the neighborhood with a camera will quickly yield a film roll full of useful textures. From ploughed fields to manhole covers to walls covered with ivy or graffiti, there are many wonderful textures that can be easily captured on film (or via digital camera) and scanned.

When scouting for textures look for even distribution of tone and color with low contrast. Close-ups often reveal interesting detail in materials such as gravel and concrete. Color is often a secondary consideration: what counts is tonal distribution. Color balance can be edited later to suit the design. Color can also be eliminated altogether if your end use is monochromatic. Conversely, a black-and-white texture photograph can be colorized for special effects.

Depth and a sense of perspective are normally good attributes for a photograph but they should be avoided when photographing textured backgrounds. The eye should read the image as a stable foundation for whatever elements appear in the foreground. In general, avoid backgrounds that scream out with bright contrasting colors that detract attention from the foreground elements.

Finding textures in photos
The textures shown here were scanned from photos similar to those you may already have on hand or could easily take.

A

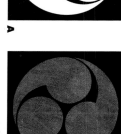

B

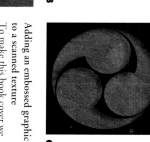

C

D

E

Adding an embossed graphic to a scanned texture
To make this book cover we began with a black and white symbol, making the white parts transparent in Photoshop (**A**). Then we added a scan of an oil painting texture on a layer below the symbol (**B**). Next we applied a drop shadow effect to the symbol layer (**C**). Now we pasted the same oil painting scan into the black areas of the symbol (**D**). Finally the bottom layer was darkened by adjusting Brightness/Contrast (**E**).

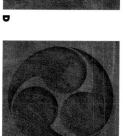
Redwood forest

Stone wall

Desert sky

Creek bed

SHINTO

FAITHS OF THE WORLD

FILLING GRAPHS WITH SCANNED PHOTO TEXTURES

Scanned photos can be used to add visual interest to otherwise dull business or statistical charts. Random or paper-derived textures can be used, but texture-filled charts are most effective when the texture has something to do with the subject of the graph. Pie charts, area charts and histograms work better with a background photo than do plot lines or scatter graphs.

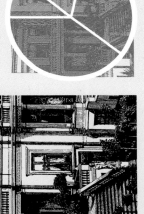

A

B

C

SALES OF ORGANIC VEGETABLES, CITRUS AND GRAINS 1980–2000

2000

1995

1990

1985

1980

Making a textured area graph
A staggered area graph was created as three layers in Photoshop (**A**). Then scans of foodstuff images were pasted into the selected area plots (**B**), applying a soft drop shadow effect to each layer (**C**).

E

F

D

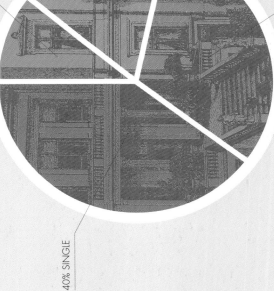

40% SINGLE

11% TWO OR MORE CHILDREN

18% ONE CHILD

32% COUPLES

Pie filling
The slices of a pie chart were given different colored fills (**D**). A line scan of urban housing (**E**) was colored grey and pasted into a circular shape on a layer above the chart (**F**). Labels complete the diagram

CREATING REPEATING PATTERNS

Scanned textures can be made into repeating patterns, similar to wallpaper, or reflected symmetrically into mandala-like designs. Both techniques are effective ways to make backgrounds that repeat infinitely. Repeated patterns can be used as screen-savers and as backgrounds for Web pages and multimedia presentations.

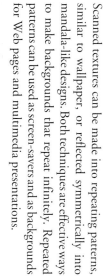

Making a mandala tile
An indifferent photo of a snowbound forest (**A**) is transformed into a design motif by repeating the image three times with successive 90-degree rotations (**B**). The resultant image can be further repeated to form a pattern (**C**).

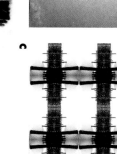

Making a seamless pattern
Rectangular images can be repeated to form an overall background. Images used in this way are known as *tiles*.

Noticeable seams where tiles meet can spoil the effect. To make a seamless tile in Photoshop, first apply the Offset filter with Wraparound selected for Undefined Areas (**D**). Then disguise the sharp edges of the seams by applying the Rubber Stamp tool (**E**).

Offset

Horizontal: 100 pixels right
Vertical: 100 pixels down

Undefined Areas
○ Set to Background
○ Repeat Edge Pixels
● Wrap Around

OK
Cancel
☑ Preview

8 Working with Scanned Photographs

Altering and Enhancing Scanned Photos

Altering Photographs
Deleting Elements
Adding Elements
Boosting Color
Changing Color

Creating Special Effects with Photos

Adding Color to Grayscale Photographs
Creating Duotones
Adding Texture to a Photograph
Morphing Between Two Photographs

Altering and Enhancing Scanned Photos

ALTERING PHOTOGRAPHS

Altering is a nice word for describing a kind of fiddling around with photographs that might also be called "distorting" or "falsifying." Photo altering has been done almost since photography was invented and some more recent incidents have become worldwide events (for example, the altering by *National Geographic* of a magazine cover photo of the Egyptian pyramids). Though such distortions have always been possible, it's much easier to alter photos on a computer than in a darkroom, so the practice is now available to anyone with a desktop system and image editing software.

THE ETHICS OF IMAGE ALTERING

Image editing makes it possible to "improve" photographs (make them more aesthetically pleasing or better suited to our purposes) by changing certain elements in ways that don't dramatically distort the meaning or veracity of the image—for example, by making the sky more blue, or by painting out a piece of trash with a sample of the surrounding grass. But we can also change photo images in more dramatic ways that do change their content and meaning and call into question the use of photographs as records of reality. Adding the head and shoulders of a board member who was absent the day the group photo was taken is a relatively benign use of image altering. Going a step further, some people ask computer artists to delete an ex-spouse from favorite family snapshots. Further still, criminals add or delete people and things from photographs presented as evidence in court. Motivations for image altering range from the convenient to the fraudulent. We'll use some rather harmless examples to show you how to alter what the camera saw, and leave it to you to use these techniques wisely.

DELETING ELEMENTS

Sometimes a good photo is marred because an extraneous person happened to walk into the background at the wrong time or perhaps there are too many cars in the scene. One of the easiest ways to delete unwanted elements from a photo is to crop it—if this can be done without also eliminating the elements you want to keep. But if cropping does not solve the problem, it's sometimes possible to use a tool like Photoshop's rubber stamp tool in Clone mode to pick up samples of the surrounding background and use them to paint over the unwanted element, so that attention is focussed on the subject. This works especially well if the background is

To crop or to clone
A photo of the organic gardens at the Stanford Inn in Mendocino was marred by a woman walking into the frame from the right (**A**). The easiest way to deal with this problem was to crop the photo to eliminate the figure. (We also improved the contrast in the photo) (**B**). However, because the unwanted figure was near areas of randomly patterned foliage it was also easy to sample these with Photoshop's rubber stamp tool and paint over the woman. This made it possible to avoid cutting off part of a cold frame in the distance, which provides important information about how the garden is managed. For our final image we also used the rubber stamp tool to remove the distracting power line (**C**).

A good memory is needed after one has lied.
—Pierre Corneille, 1642

D

E

F

Deleting and restoring

A photo of an old Buddhist temple in Mendocino suffered from poor exposure as well as a distracting padlock and a figure peering in the window on the right (**D**). Our first step in improving the photo was to increase the contrast, boost the color saturation of the bright red and green building and remove a dulling red cast from the green areas (**E**). We then used the lasso tool to carefully select the figure and delete it and used the marquee to select and delete the padlock, leaving small white shapes in the image (**F**). To fill the shapes we used the rubber stamp tool to sample adjacent areas of the window and door frames and painted into selected areas to restore the look of the original building (**G**).

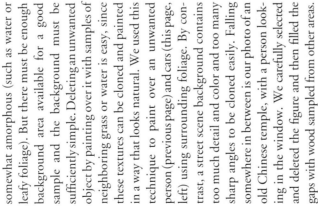

G

somewhat amorphous (such as water or leafy foliage). But there must be enough background area available for a good sample and the background must be sufficiently simple. Deleting an unwanted object by painting over it with samples of neighboring grass or water is easy, since these textures can be cloned and painted in a way that looks natural. We used this technique to paint over an unwanted person (previous page) and cars (this page, left) using surrounding foliage. By contrast, a street scene background contains too much detail and color and too many sharp angles to be cloned easily. Falling somewhere in between is our photo of an old Chinese temple, with a person looking in the window. We carefully selected and deleted the figure and then filled the gaps with wood sampled from other areas.

Removing unwanted elements

A portrait of a woman playing guitarón was marred by a group of vehicles and other distracting figures and objects (**A**). We started by improving the contrast and then used the lasso to select and then delete the unwanted elements, making especially careful selections around the pegs of the guitarón (**B**). We used the wand tool to select each white area, used the rubber stamp tool to sample areas of the background nearby and then painted into the selections to confine changes to those areas. We used the rubber stamp again to soften the edges between the new areas and the original photo (**C**).

A

B

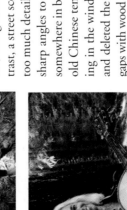

C

Appearances are deceptive.

—Aesop, 550 B.C.

ADDING ELEMENTS

One of the most exciting ways to alter a photograph is by adding elements taken from another image. This is relatively easy when the new element is added right on top of the original image. With a little more effort the new item can be layered into the existing image so that it appears in front of some parts of the original image and in back of others. In either case, it's important that the lighting, color palette, and highlights and shadows of the new material are similar to that in the original. Your composite image will immediately look faked if one object has shadows cast by a light source on the left, for example, and another has shadows cast from the right. However, if the images are similar enough, making careful adjustments to tonal range, edge blending, saturation and so on will work to make a combined image look like an unaltered original.

Redefining the truth

We started with a photo of John Odam shooting photos with his digital camera in San Francisco (**A**). Just for fun we added two members of Janet Ashford's family to the scene: her brother Doug Isaacs (**B**) and her daughter Florence Ashford (**C**), both holding cameras. The photos were good candidates for combining because all three had been taken outdoors on overcast days and were similar in shadowing, skin color and tonal range. We used the lasso to silhouette the figures of Doug and Florrie and pasted them into the scan containing John, each into its own layer so that they could be manipulated separately. We edited the figures to make their contrast and saturation match that of the original photo and softened the edges of figures by applying a slight blur. We then experimented with placement and size, putting Florrie in the foreground and placing Doug further back on the sidewalk. Since Doug appeared to be taking a picture of a blank, boarded-up window, we selected a tapestry of The Virgin of Guadelupe from an Los Angeles street scene (**D**) and pasted it into the window shape, using the Skew function to make it fit. The result is a comical image of three friends who were hundreds of miles apart when their images were captured, providing a wry comment on the art of photography (**E**).

A

B

C

D

E

E

F

BOOSTING COLOR

Sometimes a photograph is strong in content and composition but has washed out color—because the film was overexposed, or the camera was pointing toward the sun, or simply because it was an overcast day. Much can be done in an image-editing program to boost the saturation of such a photo, effecting either the whole image or selected areas. When overall thinness of color is the problem, try increasing the saturation of the entire image. When only part of the image needs correcting—for example, the white sky of a cloudy day—select that part and experiment with saturation and other controls to deepen the color or change its color components.

CHANGING COLOR

Changing a white sky to blue can change the feeling of a photo from melancholy to cheerful, without significantly changing the pictorial content of the image. It's an edit that won't be noticed by most viewers. But sometimes a more dramatic change in color is desired. Using controls for hue, saturation and selective color, it's possible to change the colors in all or part of an image so that they are completely different from those of the original. This is especially useful in advertising, fashion, package design and catalog photography, to easily create differently colored versions of the same object—for example, shoes, bicycles, or other items that come in several colors—without having to take several photographs. This technique is also useful in landscaping, architecture and interior design, so that different paint or fabric colors can be previewed.

Improving color

A photo of a Victorian mansion in San Francisco had excellent composition and interest but the contrast was poor and the colors were washed out (**A**). We used Levels in Photoshop to improve the contrast overall and then boosted color by increasing the saturation of the whole image (**B**). We used Selective Color to increase the cyan and yellow components of the greens, making the foliage brighter (**C**). We then used the rubber stamp tool to remove the distracting electrical wire and applied Unsharp Mask to sharpen and improve contrast (**D**).

A

B

C

D

G

Changing color

The outlines of the outer courtyard at the mission La Purísima Concepción, near Santa Barbara, are characteristically handsome (**E**). But the deep salmon color of some of the paint is not in keeping with the whitewash historically used on mission walls. To experiment with changing the color, we used the lasso to select just the wall areas of the bell tower and courtyard wall, leaving the other building, roof, stairs and wood trim, as well as the background landscape, unselected. The selection was saved in a channel (**F**). We then used Selective Color to repeatedly remove color from the salmon areas so that they became the same off-white color as the main mission building. All of the texture and shadowing on the walls was preserved and automatically changed in hue as the salmon color was removed. We then took the liberty of using Selective Color to transform the grass from dry summer brown to rich winter green (**G**). More variations can be seen on the opening page of this chapter.

Creating Special Effects with Photos

ADDING COLOR TO GRAYSCALE PHOTOGRAPHS

In the days before color photography, portraits and family groups were shot in black-and-white and sometimes printed as sepia-toned prints. These old photos, as well as family snapshots taken through the 1950s, were often colorized by painting directly on the photographic prints with special paints or inks. Hand-tinting added a special, subtle look to old photos, as soft smudges of pink blossomed on cheeks and robin's egg blue appeared—sometimes improbably—in eyes. Some illustrators still use the old-style photo paints to add ethereal color to black-and-white prints and this look can be duplicated electronically to add soft color to scanned photos. The color can be exaggerated to create a special effect that makes an old subject look contemporary.

Tinting by hand

Old black-and-white photographs, such as this 1940 high school graduation portrait of Janet Ashford's mother, Alice Munro, were often hand-tinted with special paints. This look can be duplicated electronically by adding color to a scanned photo in an image-editing program such as Photoshop. In the case of the two photos on this page, it's remarkable to see how much women's dress, hairstyle and demeanor changed over the course of only 40 years.

Adding color to history

We started with a scan of a photo of Janet Ashford's grandmother, Florence Scriven Munro (right) and a cousin, taken around 1900. We adjusted the tonal range in Photoshop, sharpened the image with Unsharp Mask, and converted the grayscale scan to RGB (**A**). Then, to prepare for tinting, we used the lasso tool to select areas of the image that we wanted to color (faces, lips, eyes, hair, bows, dresses and background) and saved each selection in a separate channel. (When the Channels palete is active and all the selection channels are clicked on, the on-screen image shows all the selected areas defined by differing tints of color (**B**.) We then filled each selection area in turn with a different color, placed in its own layer, and set the layer to Multiply rather than Normal mode so that the color did not change the black tones of the original. We also reduced the opacity of each color layer to levels between 35% and 64%. The result is a subtly colored portrait of two stylish young women preserved from another age (**C**).

To create a more dramatic color treatment, we started with the softly tinted version and chose the Equalize command, which turns the darkest pixels in an image to black, the lightest pixels to white and redistributes the midtone pixels between them. This increased the contrast in the photo in a way that made it look paradoxically more old-fashioned and more contemporary (**D**).

CREATING DUOTONES

If you are preparing scanned images for commercial printing in two or more spot ink colors you might consider using *duotones*. A duotone—a print made with two inks—adds depth to a photograph. (Adding more ink colors makes a *tritone*, a *quadtone*, and so on.) Photoshop provides an easy method for creating duotones. The starting image must be in grayscale mode. Selecting Duotone in the Mode menu allows you to specify ink colors. The gamma curves for each color can be manipulated to create strong or subtle effects. Since this book is printed in the four process ink colors (CMYK), we can only simulate the effect of spot color duotones on this page.

Original scan

Grayscale conversion

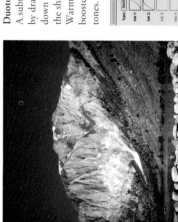

Grayscale printed in PMS 3165

Duotone: black plus a color

A subtle effect was produced by dragging the Black curve down to increase the depth of the shadows. Dragging the PMS Warm Gray 5 curve upward boosted the color in the midtones.

Duotone: complementary colors

Black need not be used as one of the two ink colors in a duotone. Black can be approximated by using two dark complementary colors. (See pages 32–33 for more about complementary colors.) We adjusted the curves in the duotone dialog box to favor the blue in the midtones and the brown in the shadows.

Tritone

A tritone adds a third ink color but looks similar to a duotone. Our curve manipulations were designed to shift the peak of each color to a different part of the tonal range, allowing each one to become dominant in some part of the image.

Printing in a single ink color (left), other than black, often makes a photo look pale and flat.

Original scan

Grayscale conversion

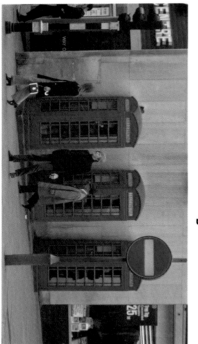

ADDING TEXTURE TO A PHOTOGRAPH

By using the many native Photoshop filters and third-party plug-ins it's possible to add an almost limitless variety of texture effects to photographs (see pages 70–71 and 92–93). But you can extend the range of possibilities even further by adding your own textures to photographs, or by using textures that have been scanned from clip art sources (see page 58). There are many ways to add texture to an image. Experiment to find the combinations that are most pleasing or effective.

Adding an overall texture
The original color scan was combined with a scanned paper texture (**A**), and a detail of brushwork from an oil painting (**B**). To achieve the texture effect we used the Overlay mode in Photoshop on the layer containing the photograph. This allowed the dynamic range of the texture scan on the lower layer to read through the photographic image above it.

Adding texture to selected areas
The gray parts of this London street scene were selected and a high-contrast scan of a piece of paper was pasted into the selection. The texture layer was set to Lighten mode and made 50% transparent to create a graphic effect.

TRANSFORMING A SCANNED IMAGE INTO A PAINTING

Painter is a unique program that simulates fine art media. Digital paintings and drawings can be created from scratch or by modifying existing digitized images. We started with a snapshot of a rock formation under a desert sky and selected sections of the original (**A**, **B**, **C**) for studies in Painter's Oil Painting, Watercolor and Van Gogh cloning brushes. We opened our source image in Painter and created a "clone," which can be either a blank canvas or "tracing paper" through which the original shows through as a pale image. As a selected clone painting tool is dragged over the virtual canvas, corresponding areas of the original are revealed, magically transformed into paint. For more examples of Painter effects see "Painting Electronically" on page 52.

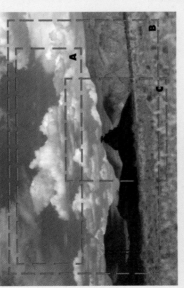
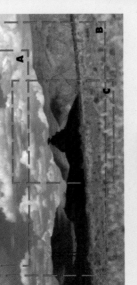

Smear and impasto
The clouds were transformed into an oil painting study using an oil painting cloner brush. After saving the cloned image the smear tool was used to smudge the edges as though with a turpentine-soaked rag.

A

Faking a Van Gogh
Vincent Van Gogh tended to mix his paint on the canvas, rather than on the palette. Painter's "Van Gogh" cloner brush takes colors from selected areas of the image and converts them into bold multicolored strokes of paint.

B

C

Simulating a watercolor
The water color cloner brush produces an effect remarkably like an on-the-spot watercolor sketch.

B

Starting and ending images with key points

MORPHING BETWEEN TWO PHOTOGRAPHS

One of the more exotic techniques available for altering photographs on desktop computers is known as *morphing*. Morphing is the blending of two different images in a sequence in which one image gradually appears to turn into the other. Using the Morph software, key points placed on a starting image appear also on the ending image. One simply drags these duplicate points from first image to match up to the outline of the second image. Morphing works best when the two photographs are similar in orientation and lighting. For example, a morph between two people wearing hats against a dark background will be more successful than one between two people, one with a hat outdoors and one without a hat indoors.

 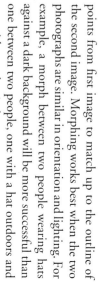

9 | Transforming Photos into Graphics

Working with High-Contrast Images

CREATING HIGH-CONTRAST IMAGES

High-contrast images are dramatic and fascinating. They reduce the continuous tones of a photographic image to areas of stark black and white that emphasize only the most crucial elements of a picture. The effect is especially striking with human faces. The shapes that make up eyes, nose and mouth—shapes that our brains are hard-wired to search for and recognize—suddenly stand out in sharp contrast to the lighter field around them, exaggerating expression and evoking strong emotional responses.

High-contrast images have been created in the conventional darkroom for many years and have become part of the visual vocabulary of design and illustration. Creating them with image-editing software is relatively simple using the tonal range functions available in most programs. One key is to adjust the midtones so that as contrast is increased (by adjusting the light and dark ends of the tonal range) there remains enough visual information to make the image readable (see "Improving Image Quality on pages 16–17 for information on midtones and basic image-editing). Another key is to edit different areas of an image separately, as we did with the image on this page.

One can also use certain filters to convert a photograph to a drawing-like image that contains only black and white (see "Applying Graphic Filters to Photos" on pages 92–93). On the opposite page we show how to add solid areas of color underneath a high-contrast black-and-white image, to create graphics in the style of Andy Warhol's silk-screened portraits (for example, of Marilyn Monroe). In addition, a dramatic effect can be created by layering a high-contrast version of a photo over a color layer containing the original photo (see "High-Contrast Images as Overlays" on page 88).

A

E

F

B

American Women in Higher Education 1900-1999

C

D

G

Increasing the contrast

To create a high-contrast image we started with a photo of Janet Ashford's mother graduating from college in the 1940s (**A**). We cropped the photo (**B**) and used Levels to exaggerate the contrast. However, as the facial features became darker, the gown lost detail and became almost solid black (**C**). Continuing to increase the contrast so that the image was completely black and white produced a dramatic image but with less detail than we wanted (**D**). So we used the lasso tool to select the face and used Levels to increase the contrast only in that area until it looked right (**E**). Then we inverted the selection to select the background and used Levels again to increase contrast in that area to a lesser degree (**F**). We applied the Median filter to smooth the image and used the rubber stamp tool to remove a crack in the original photo (**G**).

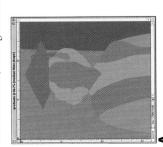

Adding a layer of solid color

To add a color background to our graduate image we used the lasso to select separate areas of the photo (such as the gown, cap, hair, and so on) and saved each selection in a channel. When the Channels palette is active and all the selection channels are made visible, a graphic image emerges as each selection area is defined by a different tint of color (**A**). In a separate layer below the one containing the photo, we loaded each selection in turn and filled it with a solid color, creating a solid color background (**B**).

Using different blending modes.

Photoshop's blending modes, available through the Layers palette, make it possible to blend different layers of an image together in various ways. By applying different blending modes to the layer containing our high-contrast black-and-white photo image (the "blend" layer) we were able to blend its areas of black and white with the solid colors in the layer below (the "base" layer), creating a variety of different effects. To start, we applied the Color Burn mode (which darkens the base color to reflect the blend color) (**C**). We also tried Multiply mode, which multiplies the base color by the blend color (**D**); Luminosity (which creates a result color that has the hue and saturation of the base color and the luminance of the blend color) (**E**), Darken (which chooses and displays whichever color in the two layers is darkest) (**F**); and Overlay (which mixes the blend colors with the base colors to reflect the lightness or darkness of the original colors) (**G**).

As a result of this graphic manipulation, all these images now have a poster-like style and present a woman who is no longer "Alice Munro" but simply "the graduate."

WHAT'S THE DIFFERENCE BETWEEN A PHOTO AND A GRAPHIC?

Photographs are usually intended to duplicate reality. Even though a photo is in fact a symbolic representation—something that only *refers* to real objects—photographs often look so realistic that they seem almost the same as the objects they represent. A graphic, on the other hand, is a more abstract visual image that definitely functions as a *symbol* or *icon*, rather than a duplicate.

Sometimes a realistic photo makes the best illustration; for example, to show the details of a particular product. But sometimes a *graphic* is more effective, especially when you're trying to convey an idea. For example, a photo of an eye presents only that particular eye (and could illustrate an article on personality), but a more abstract graphic treatment of the same eye (made by boosting contrast and adding color, above) can refer to eyes in general (and might be a better choice for an article on vision, for example).

In a graphic image, details are simplified, particulars are suggested, and nothing is strictly realistic. Image-editing software makes it relatively easy to convert photographs to symbols by performing calculations on component colors, gray values and edges so that the reduction of nature to icon is automated in a way. The key is to chose a photo that can work well as a symbol—a person in a clearly defined occupation, an object such as a flower, a hand, a house—and use editing techniques that reduce detail and increase contrast.

A

B

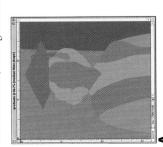

C Color Burn

D Multiply

E Luminosity

F Darken

G Overlay

There is light in shadow and shadow in light,
And black in the blue of the sky.
—Lucy Larcom, 1826–1893

HIGH-CONTRAST IMAGES AS OVERLAYS

To get the drama of a high-contrast image, but still retain the rich texture of a continuous-tone photograph, try making a high-contrast version of a color photo and layering it over a saturation-boosted copy of the original. This technique can be used to transform rather ordinary photographs into colorful, memorable images. In the case of our Victorian house image, the high contrast version looks almost like a line drawing and looks pleasant both with and without the color underlay.

Creating a high-contrast overlay

We started with a photo of a Victorian-style house in Park City, Utah (**A**) and duplicated it into another layer in Photoshop. We used Hue/Saturation on the new layer to remove the color and then applied Unsharp Mask to exaggerate the edges (**B**). We then used Levels to exaggerate the contrast, producing an image that looks almost like a line drawing of the house (**C**). A few edges were missing, so we used the pencil tool to draw them on a third layer, using the original photo image as a guide (**D**). We then combined the high-contrast and pencil drawing layers to produce a black-and-white image (**E**). We then used Hue/Saturation to increase the saturation of the original photo (**F**) and blended the black-and-white image with the color image below it, using Darken mode (**G**).

Distorting and Filtering Images

SOLARIZATION

When a photographic negative is exposed to light during the development process, the image is "fogged" resulting in a partial reversal of light and dark tones. Some of the dark areas become lighter and some of the light areas become darker, resulting in an eerie effect that's a blend between a positive and a negative image. In addition, the fogging process creates distinct lines along the edges of light and dark areas. This effect is commonly called *solarization*, though its correct name is "pseudo-solarization" or the *Sabatier effect.* Solarization can be imitated with image-editing software and can be used when you want a photographic image to look both real and "unreal."

In the conventional darkroom the solarization process involves several steps and is hard to control. As one photo manual describes, "If a photographic material is exposed, developed, washed but not fixed and then exposed to diffused light and again developed, a positive image or a combination of a positive image and a negative image is obtained…" (C. B. Neblette, *Fund. Photogr.*, 1970). The process is much easier to control in Photoshop or a similar image-editing program, either by using a Solarize filter or by editing the light and dark curves. Other interesting effects result from blending positive and negative images using different modes in Photoshop.

Blending positive and negative

We scanned a color photo of a guitar player (**A**) and solarized it using Photoshop's Solarize filter (**B**). This filter leaves half of the brightness values normal and inverts the other half, imitating the conventional darkroom solarization technique.

To show the effect more clearly, we also created a black-and-white version of the photo (**C**), and applied the Solarize filter to it (**D**). Opening the Curves dialog box after applying the Solarize filter to each image shows how the filter inverted half of the values in each (**E**).

Solarizing with Curves

After applying the Solarize filter to the color image we used Curves to edit the image curve in all three of the RGB channels, producing a dramatic effect in the image (**F**). The Curves dialog box shows how we manipulated the curve, pulling the center up to exaggerate the inversion of half the values in the image (**G**).

F

G

A

C

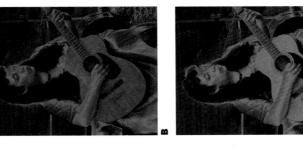

B

D

E

POSTERIZATION

The posterization process reduces the number of tonal levels or levels of brightness in a continuous-tone image, so that instead of smooth transitions from tone to tone, there are sudden jumps between tone levels, producing areas of flat color. For example, when a photographic image is scanned in grayscale mode with 256 shades of gray, and then converted to a 4-level posterization, the posterized image contains only 4 different shades of gray. Posterization dramatically converts a photo into a "graphic" by converting areas of photographic detail into tone-filled shapes that are more similar to what a graphic artist might produce when rendering a scene with ink wash or crayon. Posterization is done in the darkroom by using color filters or by varying exposure times to create a number of different negatives, each of which contains areas of a single tone. These are combined into a master negative and printed. Photoshop makes the process easy by providing a Posterize command. With it, the brightness value of every pixel in the original is analyzed and converted to the nearest of the brightness levels you specify. Any number of brightness levels between 2 and 255 can be specified and will be equally spaced between white and black. The fewer the number of levels, the more dramatic the results.

When a color image is posterized through Photoshop, the results are a little different than for grayscale images. Photoshop creates the specified number of tonal levels (or brightness values) for each channel in the image. So for an RGB image, for example, choosing a level of 4 in the Posterize command would create twelve different tones (four for each of the three channels). Though not as straightforward as with black-and-white, posterizing a color photo can create very interesting and graphically satisfying effects.

*When the Many are reduced to One,
to what is the One reduced?*

—Zen koan

A

B

C

D

E

Posterizing a continuous-tone image

We scanned a photo of fruits and vegetables and converted it to grayscale mode. The gradient bar below the photo shows the 256 levels of gray contained in the scan, which appear to blend smoothly from black to white (**A**). We used Photoshop's Posterize command to specify a 4-level posterization, which converted both the image and the gradient bar to four gray levels (**B**).

To show how posterization affects a color image, we used the color photo and added a rainbow-like bar (copied from one of Photoshop's color palettes) with smooth transitions between the colors (**C**). We then specified a 4-level posterization. The myriad colors in the original photo and bar were converted to a smaller number of hues so that there are four brightness levels in each of the three channels of the RBG image (**D**).

Finally, we started with the original color scan, applied the Median filter to smooth our variegated areas, specified a 6-level posterization and then boosted the saturation to create a brightly colored graphic treatment (**D**).

Art is the imposing of a pattern on experience, and our esthetic enjoyment in recognition of the pattern.
—Alfred North Whitehead, 1953

A

D

B

C

E

F

CREATING A SILK-SCREENED LOOK

Artists use paint and a good eye to reduce the broad tonal range they see in landscapes and other scenes into dramatic areas of flat poster-like color. But with an image-editing program we can take a shortcut to similar results by starting with a scanned photograph to create a posterization that imitates an artist's style. We scanned a photo and used Photoshop to boost its color saturation and then reduce it to a 6-level posterization, producing a graphic with the look of a sophisticated silk-screen print. One of the keys to this technique is careful preparation of the image both before and after posterization. We applied the Dust & Scratches filter to reduce noise before applying the Posterize command and afterward we applied the Median filter to smooth the edges of the color areas created by the posterization process. Though we started with a rather lackluster photo of a beautiful coastline, our cropping and posterization produced a handsome illustration that looks similar to a hand-pulled silk-screened poster.

Making a poster

We started by scanning a slightly overexposed photo of the California coast near Fort Bragg (**A**). We rotated the photo slightly in Photoshop so that the horizon was level and cropped it so that the fence descending to the beach more dramatically draws the eye of the viewer from the foreground to the ocean (**B**). We then used Hue/Saturation to increase the saturation, producing a slightly "hyper" real version with bright shades of blue, yellow and green (**C**). To prepare for posterizing, we applied the Dust & Scratches filter to reduce the amount of "noise" in the image; for example, the many small areas of color in the ground cover plants and in the water (**D**). We then specified a 6-level posterization, which reduced all the color tones in the original to just 18 levels of brightness (see explanation of the posterization process on the opposite page) (**E**). We then applied the Median filter to smooth away some small, rough color shapes created by the posterization. The finished electronic poster, with type added, looks quite similar in style to those produced traditionally by the silk-screen method (**F**).

APPLYING GRAPHIC FILTERS TO PHOTOS

Image-editing filters are sets of mathematical calculations designed to distort images in particular ways. Filters can be used to apply special effects to images in ways that enhance their graphic quality. For example, photographs can be instantly converted to "paintings" by using an appropriate filter. Photoshop includes many filters, which are grouped into categories that include Artistic, Blur, Brush Stroke, Distort, Noise, Pixelate, Render, Sharpen, Sketch, Stylize and Texture. In addition, a number of software developers have created plug-in filters than can be used with Photoshop and similar image-editing programs. Within Photoshop the Artistic, Brush Stroke, and Sketch filters are among the best for transforming scanned photographs into images that have interesting graphic qualities, but without overly distorting the content of the photo.

Most of the filters shown here were used at their default values, but most include two or more parameters (such as amount, edge intensity, cell size, light and dark balance) that can be adjusted to produce different effects, so an infinite variety of images can be produced. One can also alter the effect of a filter by applying it when a channel containing a solid gray tone is selected, so that the filter works at a percentage of its full strength. In addition, placing a black-to-white gradient in a selection channel will cause a filter to be applied gradually across an image (see opposite page). By adjusting parameters, or by using a selection mask, or by applying several filters in succession, very rich variations can be created.

Original image

Artistic, Colored Pencil

Artistic, Cutout

Artistic, Fresco

Artistic, Paint Daubs

Artistic, Poster Edges

Artistic, Smudge Stick

Artistic, Sponge

Artistic, Watercolor

Brush Strokes, Crosshatch

Brush Strokes, Dark Strokes

Brush Strokes, Spatter

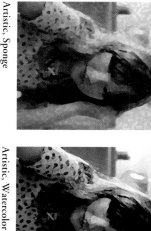

Brush Strokes, Sprayed Strokes

Distort, Diffuse Glow

Distort, Ripple

Noise, Add Noise

Pixelate, Mosaic

APPLYING A FILTER THROUGH A GRADIENT MASK

To create a special effect we created a black-to-white gradient in an alpha channel in Photoshop and applied it to our original image as a selection. We then applied the Charcoal filter (from the Sketch collection). Areas that were masked by the black part of the channel were protected from the effects of the filter, while areas that were white allowed its full strength effect. In between, the gray areas of the mask allowed the partial effect of the filter, increasing gradually from left to right. The same technique was used to alter the photo on the cover of this book.

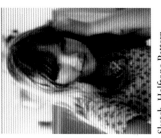
Sketch, Halftone Pattern

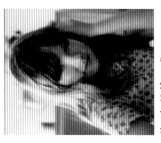
Sketch, Conté Crayon

Sketch, Charcoal

Sketch, Chalk & Charcoal

Sketch, Water Paper

Sketch, Torn Edges

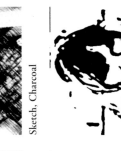
Sketch, Stamp

Sketch, Photocopy

Stylize, Wind

Stylize, Glowing Edges

Stylize, Find Edges

Stylize, Emboss

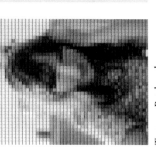
Texture, Patchwork

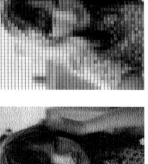
Texture, Texturizer, Canvas

Texture, Grain, Speckle

Texture, Grain, Contrasty

DEALING WITH FILTER DISTORTIONS

Image-editing with an image-editing program such as Photoshop makes it possible to convert humdrum snapshots into more interesting and artistic images, opening up a new world of special effects for portrait photography. In particular, applying graphic filters is an easy, enjoyable and powerful way to add interesting effects. The randomly placed background elements that often clutter up casual people shots can sometimes be transformed by filters into beautifully textured areas with painterly interest.

But watch out—the same filter that enhances a background can make the faces of family and friends look like creatures from outer space. One solution is to mask the faces and other areas of skin in a photo and then to apply the filter only to the background elements, leaving the skin areas untouched. Depending upon the filters used, this can produce an effect almost like that of the paintings of Gustav Klimt, in which the warmly modeled flesh tones of faces, arms and hands are contrasted with hard, flat textured areas of clothing and background.

From photo to painting
Photo portraits can be converted to painterly images by carefully selecting image filters (see pages 92–93) to find ones that create artistic effects without distorting faces in unpleasant ways. We used Photoshop's Colored Pencil filter to transform a mundane photo of a girl at summer camp into an affecting portrait. Cropping the image also helped to focus the composition.

A **B** **C** **D** **E**

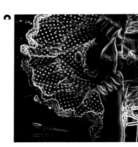

F

Saving Face
Some filters apply effects that distort faces beyond recognition. To avoid this, we used Photoshop's polygon lasso tool to select the face, hair and arms of a sassy girl (**A**), clicking from point to point around the shapes. The selections were saved in a single channel and then inversed so that when the channel was loaded, the skin areas were protected from the action of the filters or other editing (**B**). After loading the selection, we applied a fairly deep feather (8 pixels on a 688-pixel wide image) to soften the transition between filtered and unfiltered areas. Because the photo has strong emotional as well as graphic content, the altering of the background using a bold filter such as Glowing Edges added to the mood without overpowering the subject. But notice how the filter created a *girl-from-space* look when applied to the entire image (**C**). The image looks better when the filter is applied only to the background areas, leaving the face unchanged (**D**). We experimented with two other filters: the Sumi-e filter created soft black strokes along edges (**E**) while the Underpaint filter made the background areas blur. We boosted the saturation after using this filter (**F**).

Auto F/X PhotoGraphic Edges No. 59.

Auto F/X PhotoGraphic Edges No. 126 (inset and No. 115 (outset).

ADDING EDGE EFFECTS

In the early days of photography, the hand application of emulsion to glass plates resulted in uneven edges. In these days of digital perfection we can recreate this antique effect to add character to an image.

The examples on this page were made with Auto F/X, a Photoshop plug-in providing hundreds of different edge treatments. Edge Effects may be applied as Outset (extending beyond the edges of the image) or Inset (extending inward from the edges) or in combination (extending both inward and outward. Different background colors create even more possibilities.

Creating a black border

A black border was added to the image by enlarging its canvas size in Photoshop with black as the background color. Then the black border was given an edge effect treatment by applying an outset edge effect to the border, but leaving the image area intact.

Choosing a black background

One way to dramatize a photograph is to select a black background when applying an edge effect.

Creating Photo Montage Illustrations

COMBINING IMAGES

A *montage* is an illustration in which realistic components are combined to form an abstract design. Objects may be out of scale with each other or may form unusual spatial relationships. The juxtaposition of images in unexpected, bizarre ways can produce the quality of a dream, in which seemingly incongruous images coexist. It's left up to the beholder to unravel the meaning.

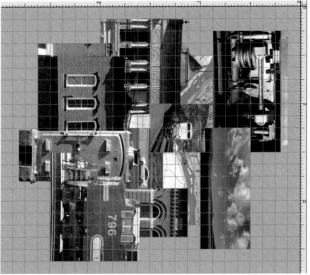

Using grids and layers
A rail trip through New Mexico supplied the raw material for this montage. Cropped scans were pasted into layers, and moved into various trial positions. Changing the order of the layers altered the composition and making Photoshop's grid visible made it easier to fine-tune the positions of the different elements.

Using free association
We gathered together scans that happened to be lurking on a hard drive and copied and pasted them into Photoshop to produce this fortuitous collage.

Using semi-transparency
The monochrome architectural photo has the Hard Light blending mode applied to its layer. This allows the dark areas of the image to darken and the light areas to lighten the fabric image on the lower layer.

Using selective transparency
In this montage study for a psychology book cover the sky image has been allowed to bleed into the dark areas of a stairwell.

USING TRANSPARENT LAYERS

There are two basic ways to approach a montage. The images can be opaque and overlapping (*decoupage* is another name for this style), or they can be in transparent layers, much like a double exposure onto film.

The first step in creating a montage in transparent layers is to find a set of photographs that fit well together. They may share a common theme, such as boats, animals, buildings, or people, or they may have color, texture or a mood in common. To keep it simple, limit the originals to three or four.

Having made your choice, now completely ignore the meaning of the images and look for rhythm and shape. Turn them upside down, rotate, crop and scale them until the composition begins to take shape. Look for matching alignments, such as horizons or windows, and play with butting and overlapping elements so that one set of shapes flows into another. Let the outside boundaries of the cluster of images be irregular if necessary, rather than force everything into a tidy, square frame. Allow accidental phenomena, like crooked scans or torn edges to influence the direction the montage takes as it develops.

CREATING LAYERS OF MEANING

Photomontages are a widely-used graphic style in advertising and editorial art. Apart from their abstract visual quality, montages can convey specific ideas in a way that other media techniques cannot. Sometimes a topic is too broad to be represented by a single image; in other cases there is a conflict, contrast or dichotomy that can be conveyed by the juxtaposition of two or more images.

Contrasting scales
A cosmic collision of galaxies and a woman's profile implies an interesting affinity between physics and metaphysics.

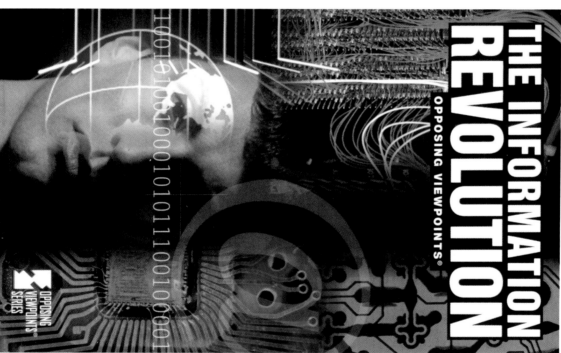

Combining images with feathered selection
In this book cover details of digital technology artifacts—circuits, cables and chips—are superimposed on a slightly bewildered human face. Feathering the edges of the images smooths the transitions.

Making a visual pun
Combining two objects of similar shapes is sometimes a powerful way of making a point. A photograph of the top of New York's Chrysler building, for example, might be combined with a photo of an ear of corn to make an editorial statement about urban and rural cultures. In the example above, a photo of a bomb was combined with a globe to suggest the concept of "weapons of mass destruction."

10 | Creating Type Treatments

Using Old Typefaces

TYPE FROM HISTORICAL SOURCES

Your scanner can be used not only to capture photos and other graphic images, but to extend the range of the typefaces you use. Type can be scanned from your original drawings or from old type specimen books. Unlike artwork, typefaces are not protected by copyright, much to the dismay of type designers. Only the *name* of the typeface is protected! You may not scan Helvetica, for example, convert it to a font and market it under the name of Helvetica (although you could if you called it "Swiss Sans," for example).

There are two basic ways to handle scanned type: Either use individual scanned characters as graphics for initial caps or to compose short headlines, or generate a font using a typographic program so that you can type the font characters from the keyboard.

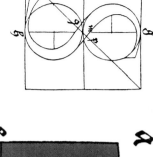

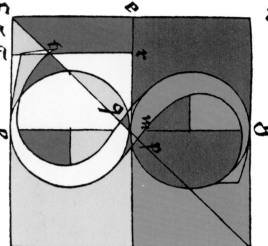

Transforming a letter scan
An example of the letter "S" by Albrecht Dürer, 1535 shows the underlying geometry of the letterforms originally created by the Roman stonecutters. Graphic transformations might include adding solid color to areas of the design, and applying an embossing filter.

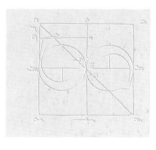

Initial capital letters from the Renaissance
A 12th century capital scanned from *Illuminated Initials* (Dover 1995) forms a delightfully sinuous design. We scanned the ½-inch letter, autotraced and converted it to PostScript to allow it to be enlarged without getting too fuzzy. Color was added in FreeHand.

Creating an initial cap
An anthropomorphic initial scanned from *Old Fashioned Silhouettes* (Dover, 1988), forms the basis of a colored drop cap for a page layout.

OUR SCORE and seven years ago our fathers brought fourth, upon this continent, a new nation, conceived in liberty, and dedicated to the proposition that all men are created equal. ¶ Now we are engaged in a great civil war, testing whether our nation, or any nation so conceived and so dedicated, can long endure. We are met on a great battlefield of that war. We have come to dedicate a portion of that field as a final resting place for those who here gave their lives that great nation might live. It is altogether fitting and proper that we should do this. ¶ But in a larger sense we cannot dedicate—we cannot consecrate—we cannot hallow this ground. The brave men, living and dead, who struggled here, have consecrated it far above our poor power to add or detract. The world will little note, nor long remember, what we say here, but we can never forget what they did here. It is for us, the living, rather, to be dedicated here to the unfinished work which they who fought here have thus far so nobly advanced.

He who first shortened the labor of Copyists by device of Movable Types was disbanding hired Armies, and cashiering most Kings and Senates, and creating a whole new Democratic world: he had invented the Art of printing.

—Thomas Carlyle, *Sartor Resartus* (1833–1834)

CONVERTING SCANNED LETTERS TO POSTSCRIPT FONTS

Of the innumerable of typefaces designed since Gutenberg, many are suitable for scanning and converting to computer fonts. But since the process is tedious, it's worth checking computer type catalogs first to see if the typeface you want, or something similar, is already available from a font supplier.

CONVERSION BY AUTOTRACING

Most font-creation programs have an autotracing feature that instantly converts a scanned letter to an outline (the demonstration fonts in this chapter were made with Fontographer). The process is imprecise, however, and works best with fonts that in their original form have irregular outlines.

Autotracing a font
San Diego calligrapher Lloyd Kirkpatric gave us a sketch of this handsome original alphabet to test the feasibility of a computer-generated font (**A**). The poor quality of the photocopy gave the crisply executed typeface a "distressed" appearance—ideally suited for autotracing.

For autotracing, the scanned letters need only have a resolution of about 72 ppi, at about a 1-inch height. Each letter must be copied to the Scrapbook or Clipboard individually and pasted one by one into the template layer of the font program (**B**). If the selection rectangle for each copied character is the same size, then letters will not need to be re-scaled in the template.

Kerning pairs must be specified (**C**) to ensure that different letter combinations fit together properly at headline sizes. The standard space around each character, known as the *metrics*, is also specified in this window.

ABCDEFG
HIJKLMNP
QRSTUVW
XYZ &

A

B

Metrics from Gazette-Roman

AWKWARD AVATAR

C

CONVERSION BY HAND-TRACING

Hand-tracing—that is, using hand-and-mouse to drive software tools to trace the outline of a letter—is the best method to use when the original letters have sharp, precise edges, straight lines or delicate serifs. Any letter shape can be broken down into straight line segments and curves that can be constructed with the font-creating software in much the same way as with any other PostScript drawing program. Creating a font this way is an exacting process requiring patience and an ability to focus on details. Stroke widths have to be constant. Each letter has to be checked against every other for consistency. It's a challenge to create even a relatively simple sans serif typeface with mostly straight lines. A serif font involves even more attention to detail and careful checking for consistency.

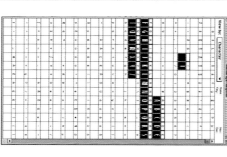

These stylish capital letters construe 26 out of the 238 characters that make up a complete typeface. Our demonstration font is Maharaja, taken from *Condensed Alphabets* (Dover 1986).

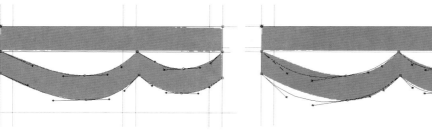

Hand-tracing a letter
A scanned letter was placed on the Template layer, just below the drawing layer where the PostScript points are established. For maximum efficiency and ease of printing, aim to use as few anchor points as possible to define the shape of a letter.

Tweaking the curves
Adjusting the Bézier control handles brings the outline into conformity with the template.

Creating New Typefaces

CREATING AN ORIGINAL CAPS FONT

Creating a clean, well-designed new typeface is an ambitious undertaking which requires quite a bit of time. But sometimes a font that's intentionally sloppy is just what you need. Deliberately weird and marginally readable fonts have found acceptance recently, especially in youth-oriented media such as MTV and skateboarding magazines. In this spirit, we created a "grunge" alphabet by using an X-Acto knife to cut letterforms from sliced potatoes. After selecting and cutting each letter to the clipboard and pasting the scanned letters into the font software's template layer, we autotraced each letterform to preserve the ragged edges of the original.

Slicing a font
The trusty X-Acto knife is the right tool for making a quick master sketch alphabet of cut paper for scanning. The "C" shape, made by cutting into a quartered potato, was the dominant form for the letter shapes, used in combination with a straight "I" shape. The potato slices were pressed onto an inked sponge pad, printed on paper and—after drying—scanned. The potatoes evolved into a font which, although crude, has rhythm and energy.

SCANNING PENCIL DRAFTS FOR A NEW FONT

As you work with redrawing historical fonts, you may gain confidence to try designing a typeface from scratch. A complete typeface is quite complex, especially if it includes both upper and lowercase characters, punctuation, numerals, ligatures, accents and special symbols. In addition, there are the different weights (bold, extra bold and so on) and italics to consider.

You don't have to draw the whole font by hand. A sketch of selected key characters can be scanned to form a template to create the complete alphabet. The lowercase "h" is a good starting point. It's relatively easy to draw and it determines the relationship of the thick and thin strokes, the ascenders and the x-height. By cutting,

pasting and modifying, the "h" forms the basis for the lowercase "n," "i," "j," "l," "m," "n," and "r." The next letters might be "d," "b," and "q," from which the "o," "a," "e" and "c" can be derived. Some letters are tricky: the "g" and "s," for example, are full of exacting curves.

After the whole alphabet has been developed, extensive testing for consistency, spacing and kerning is necessary before your font is ready to leave the nest. Because there are so many fonts on the market, each with its own identification number, be sure to check your font design software manual on how to avoid ID conflicts with other fonts. Always include your special font when sending files to your service bureau; better yet, convert all but the smallest type to outline.

Starting with a pencil sketch
Celtic letterforms in the style of a classic sans serif font were the inspiration for this project. Using traditional design tools—pencil, circle templates, french curves and tracing paper—the basis of a typeface began to emerge.

Checking the specifics
A Fontographer printout of a specific character gives detailed information about each Bezier curve and point. To ensure smooth lettering, use as few points as possible to form each character (**A**).

The still incomplete font was tested at different weights. "Hamburgerfonts" is a traditional test word in type design (**B**).

Using your font
The finished font was used to create a typographic logo for an Irish import business, fitting the business and the font nicely together (**C**).

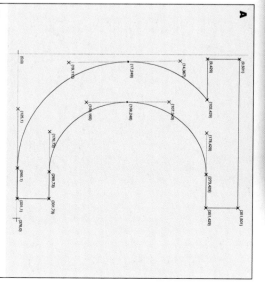

C

A

B

A FONT FROM SCANS OF YOUR OWN HANDWRITING

If you are looking for a truly original script font, you may already have designed it. Your handwriting is a typeface that has evolved over a lifetime and is uniquely expressive. To get your writing from pen and paper into font form via the scanner is relatively straightforward using a program such as Fontographer.

Here are some considerations: Put plenty of space between the letters when you write your sample so that each letter can be selected separately (don't attempt to join the letters). Remember to include punctuation. Don't fuss with the letters after they have been autotraced, trying to make them "perfect." Leave the quirks intact: those are the very attributes that make your handwriting font distinctive.

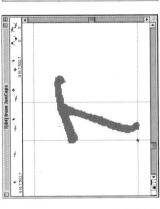

Scrapbook

Item: 17 of 108
Type: picture
Size: 2K

Dimensions: 33 by 45 pixels

A

B

C

Selecting each character

After an alphabetical sample of handwriting had been scanned, the letters were selected and pasted one by one to the Scrapbook (**A**). An image from the Scrapbook was pasted into the template layer of a character window (**B**) and autotraced (**C**). The process was repeated until the font was complete.

Establishing spacing

In Fontographer the only part of the process of converting handwriting to a font that requires skill, judgment *and* good luck is the determination of the metrics, or the amount of lateral space around each letter. Because not all letters are the same width (an "M" for instance is much wider than an "I"), each one must be treated separately. The initial state of a letter—the "O" in his case—has wide spacing around it (**D**). (The spacing of the other letters has already been set.) By dragging the right-hand vertical to the left (**E**), we established the correct distance to a following letter.

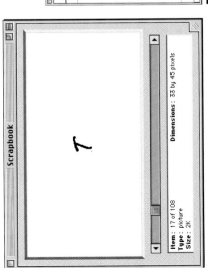

D

E

As Athenodorus was taking his leave of Caesar, "Remember," said he, "Caesar, whenever you are angry, to say or do nothing before you have repeated the four-and-twenty letters to yourself."
—Plutarch (46–120 A.D.), *Roman Apophthegms, Caesar Augustus*

A FOUND-OBJECT ALPHABET

Type design can sometimes be a form of entertainment—an artful exercise in visual scavenger hunting. Imagine, everyday objects that could serve as letterforms for a complete font are already lying waiting in your desk drawers. All you have to do is scan them!

Found object letters are useful in logos and can make interesting initial caps. A complete alphabet with lowercase, numerals and punctuation would be almost impossible to create and not really practical since it would be difficult (as with any display font) to read paragraphs of 10-point found-object type.

For more ideas and tips on scanning found objects, see Chapter 11, "Scanning Real Objects."

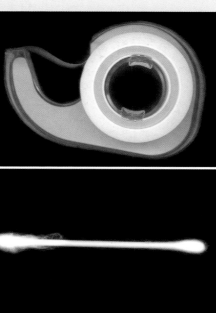

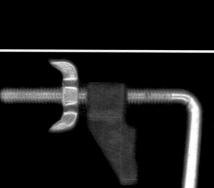

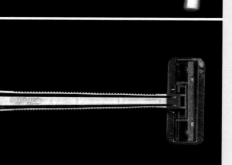

The shapes of many household objects correspond roughly to the letters of the alphabet.

A B C D E F G H I J K L M N O P
Q R S T U V W X Y Z
1 2 3 4 5 6 7 8 9 0

We found a ready-made alphabet in a box of macaroni. A bold version of the font could be made by cooking the pasta prior to scanning.

11 | Scanning Real Objects

Bypassing the Camera

"FOUND ART": SCANNING REAL OBJECTS

Sometimes the source of an original illustration is as close as that cluttered catchall drawer in your kitchen. Any object that's small and light enough to be placed on the glass of your scanner can become an instant photo image—to be used on its own or as the starting point for an illustration. By changing colors, applying filters, creating montages, or converting scanned images to line art or posterizations, you can create a variety of illustrations that are original, cheap, and readily available. (For more examples of scanning objects see "Textures All Around Us" starting on page 66).

Of course, flatbed scanners were designed for scanning flat pieces of paper. But that restriction never stopped curious people from photocopying objects and

The scanner as camera

All the images on these two pages were created by placing small items directly on the scanner glass. Each object was silhouetted in Photoshop, and drop shadows were added using Photoshop's Drop Shadow controls.

body parts on the first office copiers, and inventive designers were quick to see the potential for scanning objects when the first desktop scanners hit the market. Experimentation and an inventive mind can produce unique images that break away from the "period" look of the 19th Century clip art we describe in Chapter 5 (see "Working with Printed Clip Art" starting on page 25) or the prepackaged look of more contemporary clip art offerings.

TIPS FOR SCANNING OBJECTS

It's fun to prowl around the house, office or yard looking for objects to scan, but this kind of scanning requires some special attention.

FOCUS

With objects that have protruding parts—for example, a mask with a large nose—the background parts will be darker and less focussed than the parts that are closest to the glass. You may be able to compensate for this by editing focus and contrast in an image-editing program, or you may want to stick with objects that are flatter.

BACKGROUND

Placing a thick object on the scanner may prevent you from closing the scanner lid. The scanned object will then have a dark background, with the degree of darkness determined by the amount of ambient light in the room. You can edit out a dark background in an image-editing program (see "Removing Backgrounds" on page 22). You can also create a temporary background by placing a white box or large piece of white paper over the object, or by constructing a cover out of pieces of white foam-core board.

SHADOWS

Scanned objects will cast shadows as the scanner's light source passes across them, but these shadows don't look the same as those cast by a directional light. To achieve

more natural looking shadows, silhouette the scanned object and create a soft drop shadow in your image-editing program (see "Drop Shadows and Other Effects" on page 110).

UNWIELDY OBJECTS

Objects that are round or unbalanced may roll around or topple over on the scanner glass. Try using books or rulers to restrain your more unruly subjects. You can also use artboard, an X-Acto knife and tape to construct restraints for objects.

METALLIC OBJECTS

Because the three colored light beams (red, green and blue) from color scanners emanate at different angles, they may cause metallic objects to appear exotically multicolored when scanned. You may like the look of a rainbow-hued monkey wrench. But if not, converting the scan from color to grayscale solves the problem. Silver or steel surfaces will look quite realistic in black and white. You can add a monochrome color back to a grayscale scan to achieve the look of gold or copper. If only certain parts of an object are metallic, select these and reduce their color saturation to zero, leaving the rest of the object unchanged.

KEEPING YOUR SCANNER CLEAN

Scanners contain electrical components and are not designed for scanning liquids, though you could probably scan a fresh tomato slice if you're careful and ready to mop up the juice. Likewise, it would not be a good idea to scan dirt or flour or other fine particles that could clog the scanner's works. But we have had success scanning small things like seeds and popcorn that generate some chaff. Carefully remove such items after scanning and clean the glass with window cleaner to keep your scans dust-free. It's also possible to lay wet items on a piece of clear acetate placed on top of the scanner glass.

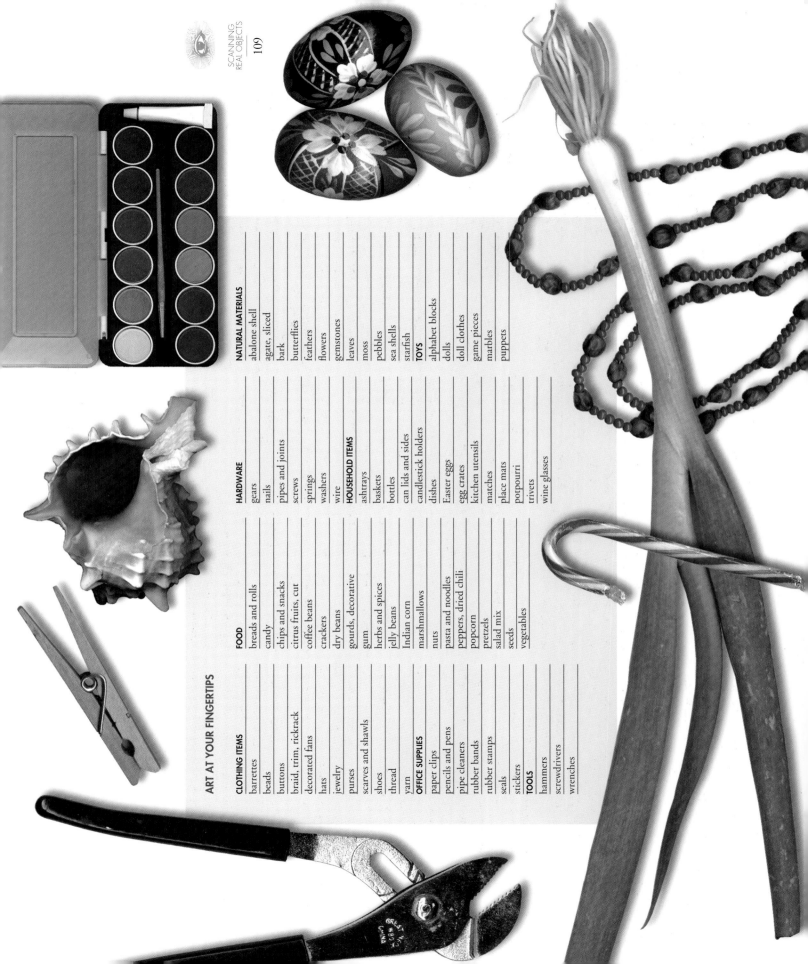

ART AT YOUR FINGERTIPS

CLOTHING ITEMS
barrettes
beads
buttons
braid, trim, rickrack
decorated fans
hats
jewelry
purses
scarves and shawls
shoes
thread
yarn

OFFICE SUPPLIES
paper clips
pencils and pens
pipe cleaners
rubber bands
rubber stamps
seals
stickers

TOOLS
hammers
screwdrivers
wrenches

FOOD
breads and rolls
candy
chips and snacks
citrus fruits, cut
coffee beans
crackers
dry beans
gourds, decorative
gum
herbs and spices
jelly beans
Indian corn
marshmallows
nuts
pasta and noodles
peppers, dried chili
popcorn
pretzels
salad mix
seeds
vegetables

HARDWARE
gears
nails
pipes and joints
screws
springs
washers
wire

HOUSEHOLD ITEMS
ashtrays
baskets
bottles
can lids and sides
candlestick holders
dishes
Easter eggs
egg crates
kitchen utensils
matches
place mats
potpourri
trivets
wine glasses

NATURAL MATERIALS
abalone shell
agate, sliced
bark
butterflies
feathers
flowers
gemstones
leaves
moss
pebbles
sea shells
starfish

TOYS
alphabet blocks
dolls
doll clothes
game pieces
marbles
puppets

DROP SHADOWS AND OTHER EFFECTS

Creating a "drop shadow" behind a silhouetted object scan is a very effective way of creating a sense of depth and making a scanned object look as though it's actually sitting on a surface. In the 1996 edition of this book we described a series of steps for creating these soft, blurred shadows. The process is much easier now that drop shadows have been automated in Photoshop, through the Layer Effects submenu. This submenu also makes it possible to create outer glows, inner glows, pillow embossing and other effects. Other image-editing programs include similar functions.

Before applying a drop shadow though, it's important to make sure that the object to be shadowed has been carefully silhouetted so that none of the background color remains along its edges. Otherwise there will be a thin line of color between the object and the drop shadow. One easy way to do this in Photoshop is to use the wand tool to select the white area around the object (after you've removed all the background elements using the techniques we describe on page 22, "Removing backgrounds") and then choose Expand from the Selection menu to enlarge the selection area by 1 or 2 pixels. This should select whatever stray pixels of color may remain along the object's edges, which you can then delete.

A

Automating shadows and effects

We started by scanning a pair of scissors (**A**) and used Photoshop's lasso tool to select the background and delete it. We then adjusted the contrast and color saturation of the red plastic handle and metal blades (B). We created a layer below the scissors, filled it with solid white and used the Layer Effects submenu to apply effects to the layer containing the scissors, including Drop Shadow (**B**), Inner Glow (**C**), Outer Glow (**D**), and Pillow Emboss (**E**). We chose black as the color for all of these shadows and effects and all were cast onto the white background layer.

B

C Drop Shadow

E Outer Glow

D Inner Glow

F Pillow Emboss

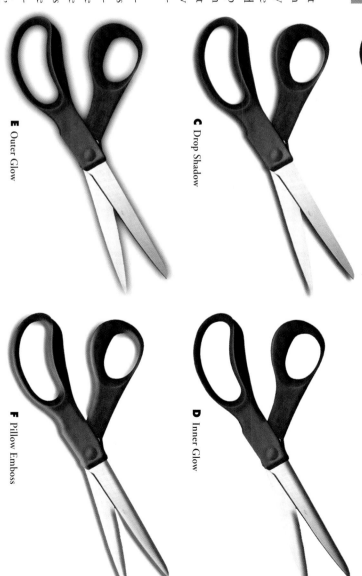

Casting shadows on color

However, an object with a shadow can also be placed in a layer above one that contains a multicolored image and the shadows will appear to be cast onto that image, as happened when we placed our drop-shadowed scissors over a scan of origami papers (**G**).

G

A MONTAGE OF OBJECT SCANS

The shapes, colors and textures of everyday objects provide a wealth of graphic ideas and scanned objects can easily be combined to create interesting montages. Unlike still-life photography, in which objects are in realistic proportion to each other, objects in a montage need not limited in this way: for example, small things can be sized to appear larger than large things. The elements of the montage on this page include: a geode, a bathtub drain, a cake decoration, a postal scale, a ceremonial corn husk, a comb, a podocarpus leaf, a scallop shell and a steel hook.

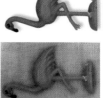

Editing the scans
To make the shape of each object stand out, murky backgrounds were deleted by making feathered selections. Consistent drop shadows were added as an effect.

Object into Graphic

SCANNING A HORN

The tendency of scanners to generate false colors in metallic objects can sometimes be used to advantage to produce slightly iridescent effects, as in our saxophone. A light green sheet was draped over the horn before scanning to create color reflections. Scanning artifacts, such as scratches on the glass and extraneous shadows add graphic character to the image.

Three-dimensional objects that are too large to fit on the scanner can, as with flat artwork, be scanned in parts and reassembled in an image-processing program. For more tips on handling large originals see page 14.

Theme and variations

We further edited our assembled saxophone scan in Photoshop to produce some interesting graphic variations. To make a CD cover we applied the Watercolor filter (**A**). In the poster below the green background and the opalescent colors on the saxophone were created by reversing (turning to negative) the cyan and yellow channels in a CMYK version of the image (**B**).

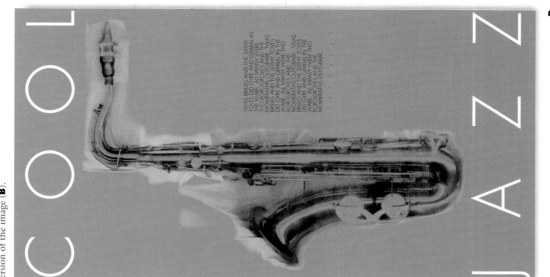

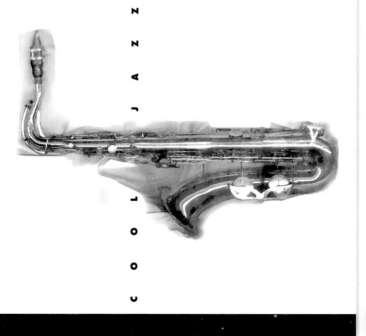

POSTERIZING AN OBJECT SCAN

Image-editing software posterizes by reducing the tonal values of either a color or grayscale image (see also "Posterization" on page 90). The process brings out hidden textures and emphasizes the abstract shapes in an object. Wood grain or metallic reflections, for example, make wonderful patterns when posterized. Posterized effects are especially useful for designs printed in a limited number of colors.

Automatic and custom posterizing
Using Photoshop's Posterize command to create a 3-level posterization produced harsh colors in the wood grain in the top of a guitar (**A**). Another method provides more control over the posterization process (**B**): In Photoshop we began by desaturating the color scan and duplicating it twice to make three identical layers. Then each layer was modified by maximizing contrast and adjusting brightness. Finally, a custom color was assigned to each layer with the Hue/Saturation control. The layers were set to Multiply.

A

B

Posterizing, blurring, and re-posterizing
The texture of a brass plumbing fixture was emphasized by a 4-level posterization in Photoshop (**C**). Applying the Median filter abstracted the color areas and posterizing again created simplified graphic shapes. (**D**). A similar effect was produced by using Gaussian Blur before posterization (**E**).

C

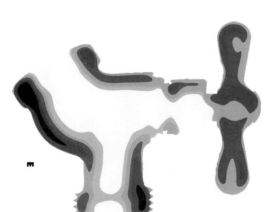

D

E

OBJECT SCAN SILHOUETTES

If you have ever taken an introductory course in photography you might have been shown how to make "photograms" —the technique of arranging objects on photographic paper, exposing it, and developing it in the darkroom. You get something of the same effect by making a line art scan an of object placed on the flatbed of a scanner.

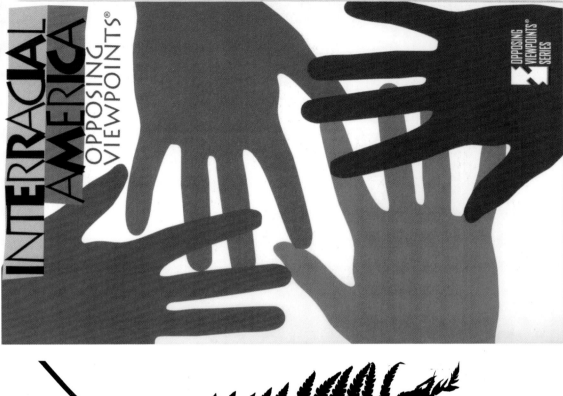

Generating shapes from found objects

Small, opaque, flat objects that have strong shapes make good subjects for scanning. The book cover (right) was made of a scan of a hand placed on the scanner. The hand scan was darkened to become a silhouette, then repeated, colored and rotated.

CONVERTING SCANNED OBJECTS INTO GRAPHICS

Image-editing tools can be used to convert a scanned object into a graphic so that it looks more like an illustration than a photograph. We were able to create an effective image by carefully balancing a real violin on the scanner glass, capturing an image, and then manipulating it to create different effects. Though we couldn't fit the entire violin into the image, the limits imposed by the 9 by 12-inch size of our scanner produced a dramatic cropping of the image.

A Original

B Increase contrast

C Chalk & Charcoal filter

D Photocopy filter

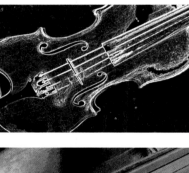

E Convert to grayscale

F Glowing Edges Filter

G Invert high contrast version

H Shift hue from blue to red

I Add black to white areas

J Increase saturation

From object to art

We started by carefully scanning a violin placed on the scanner (**A**) and used Photoshop to increase the contrast (**B**). We then applied the Chalk & Charcoal filter (**C**) and the Photocopy filter (**D**), both from the Sketch group of filters, which are used to create interesting black-white treatments of color images. We also converted the image to grayscale (**E**) and applied the Glowing Edges filter (**F**) to create another black-and-white version. Then, as a final experiment, we took the scanned violin through a number of steps. We used the Invert command to reverse the color image to a negative (**G**), and then used Hue/Saturation to shift the hue of the blue tones into the red/brown range (**H**). We then used the Selective Color command to add black to the white areas (**I**) and finally used Hue/Saturation again to increase the saturation of the entire image. We also used the rubber stamp tool to paint over some distracting striped marks that had appeared in the background of the image as it was scanned (**J**).

12 | Using Scans in Arts and Crafts

Altering and Embellishing Printed Scans

GOING BEYOND THE COMPUTER

The computer is a powerful tool for making art but it is not the only tool. The pages that come from your printer need not be the last step in your artistic process. Try thinking of your computer and printer as printmaking tools—machines that help you get interesting images onto paper, which you can work on further by hand. In this chapter we'll demonstrate a number of different ways to embellish printed output, using familiar artists' tools to color it, cut it, paste it, fold it, draw on it and in general use it as the raw material for artistic experiments.

DRAWING AND PAINTING ON LASER PRINTS

We've seen how color can be added to black-and-white art using Photoshop or a similar program (for example, see "Adding Color to Grayscale Photographs" on page 80). However, drawing or painting directly on printed output adds a special handmade touch and is an excellent way to cheaply add color to black-and-white art.

PAINTING WITH WATER COLOR

Transparent watercolors as well as gouache, an opaque watercolor, can be used to paint on laser prints. When painting be careful of buckling the paper by wetting it too much. It's sometimes a good idea to make your laser prints on heavier, more absorbent paper when you plan to paint on them later.

DRAWING WITH PENCILS AND PENS

For more subtle color it's also possible to draw on laser output with colored pencils. To avoid smudging be sure that the toner is very dry before you draw. It's probably a good idea to let your prints dry overnight. You may also want to apply a fixative to your laser prints, especially if they are printed on a textured, absorbent paper.

PAINTING BEFORE YOU PRINT

It's also possible to paint on your paper first and then print a scan on it after it's thoroughly dried.

Painting, cutting and pasting
To create illustrations for an artist's book, Janet scanned two engravings of goddesses from Dover clip art books, printed them as black-and-white laser prints and painted on the prints with gouache paint. She then cut out the figures using scissors and an art knife and pasted them with glue stick onto pieces of brown craft paper that had been previously decorated with paint and chalk. One piece was cut to a trim rectangle shape while the other was torn to add textural interest. Both illustrations were pasted onto the pages of a handmade, pamphlet-stitched book.

Printing on painted paper

Simple black-and-white line art can look very attractive when printed on paper that's been decorated beforehand. We used acrylic paints to create a marbled pattern on paper. We then scanned a quaint 18th Century woodcut from *1800 Woodcuts by Thomas Bewick and His School* (Dover, 1962) and printed it in black on top of the marbled paper. We used an illustrators' watercolor pen to paint yellow into the grasshopper's body and into the horizontal stripes at the bottom.

Editing a scan before coloring

We wanted to make a personal note card using an old family photo of Janet with her Grandma Florrie. But the background included many distracting street elements. So we started by scanning the original photo, which had been printed on deckle-edged paper (**A**). We also scanned another family photo which included trees that could function as a substitute background (**B**). The two photos were similar enough in tonal range and focus to be melded together. We cropped the grandma image and increased the contrast and focus (**C**). We then selected the background and deleted it (**D**). We then copied the other image and pasted it into a layer in the grandma image file, so that the trees showed through the two figures (**E**). We then printed the image as a black-and-white laser print on matte finish, heavyweight imaging and photo paper. We drew on the print using colored pencils and then drew a halo around Grandma using gold and silver metallic pens. We used decorative edged scissors to cut a scalloped edge around the finished card (**F**).

A

B

C

D

E

F

Creating Artist's Books

CREATING SIMPLE BOOK STRUCTURES

An artist's book combines three elements—image, text and structure—to create an art work that goes beyond the conventional printed book. Before the computer, artist books were made using handmade images combined with hand-drawn or letterpressed type and structures made from paper and board. Many artist books are still made this way, but the computer has extended the book artist's range by providing tools for producing both images and text elements that can be printed and then cut, folded or decorated further. We show examples of two of the most common book structures here: the accordion book and the stitched pamphlet. Instructions on how to create these structures, including information on stitching and making covers can be found in books on bookbinding.

ACCORDION BOOKS

Accordion books consist of a long piece of paper folded like an accordion bellows and attached to covers at each end. An accordion book can be read one page at a time or can be stood up with the pages all spread out. Some art and photo supply stores carry ready-made blank accordion books with hard covers, sized for pasting in 4 by 6-inch photo prints. These blank books can become the "structure" for an artist's book containing computer-generated images and text.

A multiple accordion book

Images of demons scanned from Dover clip art books were printed and glued into the folds of an accordion book. Another layer of folded blue and yellow paper contains the book's text. A final layer of translucent textured paper was stitched onto the outer folds with black cord. The text reads, "The anger and fear that live in the unconscious can be covered over by art and craft but cannot be destroyed."

Using both sides

To create the art for a two-sided accordion book, Janet scanned a variety of figures from various copyright-free clip art books from Dover Publications, gathering together images that express a number of personal traits. She used Photoshop to scale each image to fit her book page size, printed each in black-and-white, cut them out, and then pasted them onto the book pages together with decorative paper. The text was also created on the computer, printed, cut out and pasted. For more examples of accordion artist books created by Janet Ashford see the *Mandala Series* book on the opening page of this chapter and the *Sometimes There Is No Need for Words* book on page 64 in the chapter on textures.

QUICK TIP

For an introduction to book arts plus detailed instructions, see:

- *Cover to Cover: Creative Techniques for Making Beautiful Books, Journals & Albums* by Shereen La Plantz (Lark Books, 1995).

- *Making Books by Hand: A Step-By-Step Guide* by Mary McCarthy and Philip Manna (Quarry Books/North Light Books, 1997).

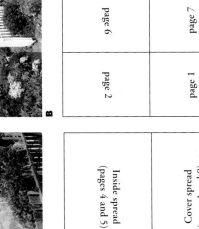

(pages 4 and 5) Inside spread	page 6	page 7
Cover spread (pages 1 and 8)	page 2	page 1

A   **B**

D

C

Books are not absolutely dead things, but do contain a potency of life in them to be as active as that soul was whose progeny they are; nay they do preserve as in a vial the purest efficacy and extraction of that living intellect that bred them.

—John Milton, *Areopagitica*, 1644

Decorating a cover

To create a decorative cover for a simple pamphlet book, Janet assembled three elements—a sun design, a piece of marbled paper and text. To create the sun element she chose a small sun stamp from a set called *Sun, Moon, and Stars Stamps*, co-published by the Metropolitan Museum of Art and Viking Press. The design is one of several taken from Renaissance stained glass, compasses and other objects in the collection of the Museum. Janet made an impression with black ink on a textured paper and then scanned the stamping at more than twice its original size. In Photoshop she increased the contrast and then applied the Add Noise filter to create a texture that made the image look slightly metallic. She printed the scan in black-and-white on a textured piece of paper, cut the print into a circle and outlined the rays of the sun by drawing with a gold metallic ink pen. To create the text she used Photoshop's type tool with the Medici Script font and printed it on the same textured paper as used for the sun. She then pasted the sun, marbled paper and text onto the front cover of a pamphlet book which she had made of folded paper and stitched together with black cord.

SIMPLE FOLDED AND STITCHED PAMPHLETS

A pamphlet is a small group of pages that have been folded and bound together by stitching with thread through the fold. A pamphlet usually contains only 8 or so pages; more pages would make it too thick to fold and stitch, though several pamphlets can be bound together into thicker books. Pamphlets can be easily made using blank paper for the inside sheets, a decorated sheet for the outside sheet, and a heavyweight paper for the cover. The cover can be decorated to create a personal blank book. The pages can also be written on or decorated to create an artist's book.

FOLD-AND-STITCH PICTURE BOOKS

This variant of the pamphlet is made by folding a single sheet of paper that has been printed on both sides and then stitching it through its center fold. These small books provide a charming way to display photos of special people, places or events.

Saving the day

To create a small 8-page picture booklet, Janet edited photos of a garden tour and assembled them in Photoshop to produce two images. The first contains the cover spread and an inside spread (**A**), while the second contains pages 1, 2, 6 and 7 (**B**), as shown in the diagrams (**C, D**). She printed the first image on a coated, heavyweight paper designed for 2-sided printing. She let the sheet dry, then printed the second image on the other side. She folded the sheet in half so that the cover spread and inside spread were on the outside and then folded again so that only the two halves of the cover spread were on the outside. She then used a metal ruler and a craft knife to trim away the white margins and the top fold of the sheets. She used a heavy needle to punch three small holes into the center fold and bound the pages together with thread using a pamphlet stitch.

Fold-and-stitch picture books provide a fast and charming way to celebrate a special place or event, such as a day at the fair, a garden party, a wedding, a walk on the beach and so on. Using a digital camera to capture the images makes the process go even faster. For more examples see page 102 of John Odam's *Start with a Digital Camera* (Peachpit, 1999).

Making Gifts and Amusements

FOLDING PRINTED SCANS

Adding a third dimension to printed scans—by folding, cutting and pasting—takes us beyond the flat page into the realm of objects. Many charming small items can be made from 8½ by 11-inch sheets and the 11 x 17-inch sheets that come from larger printers provide even more possibilities.

FOLDED ORIGAMI BOXES

Origami, the Japanese art of paper folding, is often done with decorated papers so using printed scans works well with this craft and can produce interesting effects. In addition to the well-known cranes and flowers, origami includes the creation of boxes of many shapes; we've created the cubic shape here. Remember that origami shapes always begin with a square piece of paper, so your rectangular output will have to be cut before folding.

CUT-AND-FOLDED BOXES

Going beyond the square paper, there are many Western designs for folded boxes which involve elaborately cut patterns. We scanned a press-out box from a book of press and fold boxes and scanned the back, undecorated side of it to create a template.

Creating a cubic box

We started with a scan of water lilies from a botanical garden, added color to the pink lily flowers and printed the image in color on an 8½ by 11-inch sheet of heavyweight photo imaging paper. To fold the paper into a box we trimmed it to a square and followed the instructions in *The Complete Origami Course* by Paul Jackson (Gallery Books, 1989). Origami boxes can be used to hold small items such as jewelry, potpourri, candy or party snacks.

A

B

Placing images into box shapes

To create a pair of curved boxes we scanned the back side of a punch-out jewel box and sized it to fit on an 8½ by 11-inch sheet. The box is one of many included in *The Floral Gift Boxes* by Petula Stone (Dorling Kindersley, 1992). We used the magic wand and lasso tools in Photoshop to select each of the four sides of the box and saved separate selections for each (**A**). We then created two boxes, each filled with different images. For the first box we scanned a photo of a field of flowers (**B**), pasted it into a file containing the template, and deleted the part of the image that falls outside the selection areas. We then selected the three smallest sides and used Selective color to change the color of the flowers from yellow to orange, red and pink (**C**). For the second box we scanned four photographs of ornate doors from mission-style buildings in San Diego, Los Angeles and Santa Barbara. We pasted a different door into each of the four sides of the box (**D**).

C

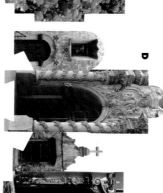

E

Folding the boxes

We cut out the flower box shape and the door box shape and folded each one. Each has one tab for glue to close the sides of the box and two slits to hold the lid tab (**E**). Small boxes such as these can be used to package small gifts or to hold small treasures.

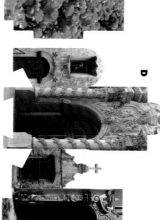

D

Going beyond checkers

To create a Nine Men's Morris board game, we started by scanning two Celtic ornaments from *The Grammar of Ornament* by Owen Jones (Dover, 1987) (**A**). In Photoshop we converted the color scan to grayscale and increased the contrast. We then autotraced them in Streamline and opened the autotracings in Illustrator to create a decorative game board design, based on the diagram for Nine Men's Morris included in *Favorite Board Games Your Can Make and Play* (Dover, 1990) (**B**).

To make a usable game board you could divide your design into quarters, print each on a single sheet of paper, then cut and glue them to a piece of poster board. Or try buying an inexpensive set of checkers and paste your color prints onto the folded game board. The checker pieces can be used with the new game. The finished design could also be printed and framed as an art piece (**C**).

A

B

NINE MEN'S MORRIS PLAYING-BOARD PATTERN

C

CREATING PHOTO DISPLAYS

A special, whimsical way to display family photos is to create a home "altar," composed of shots of friends and family combined with scanned photos of your home and surroundings, places you've visited, spiritual symbols or figures, or special items or mementos. Scanned photos can be cut and pasted onto heavy paper or lightweight board and combined with other small objects to create a focal point in your home for remembering loved ones or for celebrating the seasons and holidays of the year.

Altars for family photos

To create a family altar, Janet scanned a photo of herself and her two daughters and pasted it onto colored pa per. A paper tab pasted onto the back was folded to help the photo card stand u p. She also scanned three photos of the flowers, forest and ocean near her home, pasted these on colored paper and applied a folded backing of poster board to create a bendable triptych background. The two elements were placed on a sheet of marbled paper and two small candles were added. Altars such as this one are similar to the ones that adorn many homes in Mexico and can be also be made using scans of real objects (for example, family toys or mementos).

ALTERING PLAYING CARDS

The decks published by the U.S. Playing Card Company feature picture cards with designs similar to those published in England at the end of the 19th Century. These century-old designs can be altered in a charming way by placing the faces of family members and friends into the spaces occupied by the sternly drawn royalty.

Creating a Daughter of Hearts

Janet scanned a photo of her daughter Florrie and also a Queen of Hearts card from a drugstore deck. She selected Florrie's face, pasted it into a layer above the card, flipped it, then used the lasso to select and delete sections of the card so that Florrie fit right inside the outline of the Queen's face. This card image could be printed and framed as a small poster or could be printed on card stock at a smaller size and cut out for use as a playing card, along with face cards containing the faces of other friends and family members.

MAKING CUSTOM BOARD GAMES

Nine Men's Morris, the Game of Goose, Steeplechase, Ludo, Draughts—these are just a few of the games that originated in ancient times but are rarely played today. You can create your own designs for these amusements by following the guidelines in books on games. We transformed a drugstore checkers set into a handsome Nine Men's Morris game, using scans of old Celtic designs.

Scanning related art

To create the color art for our stationery set we scanned three different designs from Syria (Aleppo, ca.1600) from *Treasury of Historic Folk Ornament in Full Color* (Dover, 1996). We used Photoshop's Median filter to remove the moiré patterning that resulted from scanning printed material.

DESIGNING CUSTOM STATIONERY

A set of hand-folded and cut stationery will take some time to create, but makes a lovely gift for a special person. We based our set on the Baronial or invitation-size envelope (5¾ by 4⅞ inches) because all of it's elements can printed on 8½ by 11-inch sheets. We created an envelope with a patterned interior, a stationery sheet, a note card, and a folded greeting card. The letter sheets, cards and envelopes can be printed with a name and address if you wish or left blank. For more ideas see the section on business identities.

An infinite variety of scanned images can be used to decorate the elements of a stationery set. Leaf through the pages of this book for ideas. Possibilities include scans of photographs (such as flowers, greenery, sky, ocean, faces, and so on), textures or cloth (see Chapter 7, Creating Textures and Backgrounds starting on page 57), decorated paper, or your own paintings and drawings. You can also scan patterns from color clip art books of marbled paper or tartans or ethnic patterns, but watch out for moiré patterns when scanning from printed pages (see "Eliminating Moiré Patterns" on page 24). We used elements of three different designs from 16th Century Syria which are related in style and color palette.

Creating the stationery elements

We used the three Syrian designs each in slightly different way. For the letter sheet we selected the right part of one design and lightened it so that the art was pale enough to write over. To create the note card we selected a border from the same design and printed it on a textured card weight stock. To create the folded greeting card we printed another of the Syrian designs on matte paper, cut it with an art knife, and glued the art to a folded card made from the same textured card stock. The lining for the envelope was taken from a third Syrian design.

Creating an envelope

We unfolded a Baronial size envelope and scanned it to create a template (**A**). We opened the scan in Photoshop and used the lasso tool to draw around the edges of the envelope to create a selection. We added a stroke to the selection to provide an outline that we could use later as a cutting guide. We then drew a smaller selection area inside the outer selection and pasted our decorative Syrian art work into it (**B**). We printed the envelope art on a color printer, cut it along the guidelines, folded it carefully and glued it with a glue stick

13 | Scanning for the Web

The Screen Versus the Page

The Elements of a Web Page

Using Scans On-line

Optimizing Scanned Images for the Web
Developing An Organizational Web Site
Making a Family Web Site
Making Web Animations with Scans

The Screen Versus the Page

THE ELEMENTS OF A WEB PAGE

The World Wide Web—with its information, products, entertainment and causes—has become a cultural phenomenon; a vast marketplace open to anyone with access to a computer, either as a viewer or a producer.

Creating graphics for a Web page involves arranging three basic elements: text, images and backgrounds. Images can be still or animated; backgrounds can be solid colors or repeated ("tiled") images. Text and images can provide information and also serve as buttons that viewers click to link to different parts of the site or to other Web sites. In addition to simple vertical ordering of these elements, text and images can be contained within tables where they are arranged in side-by-side columns and rows.

While it's possible to program a web page using HTML (Hyper Text Markup Language) code only, it's far easier to use a Web-authoring program such as Dreamweaver, PageMill or GoLive. Such programs make it possible to arrange text and graphics on pages in the same visual, intuitive way as in a page layout program—while the HTML code that makes the page work is automatically written by the program. When a Web site is complete, all the images files and HTML page files are uploaded to a Web server, through which they become available to the Internet community.

PREPARING IMAGES FOR THE WEB

From its origins as a text-based computer network, the Web has evolved into an image-driven medium. But pictures take more time than text to travel through telephone lines, cables and computer hubs to finally appear on-screen. Scanning can be a springboard for imaginative Web graphics, provided you work within certain constraints.

RESOLUTION AND SIZE

The standard for on-screen graphics is 72 pixels per inch, the resolution of most computer monitors. But while monitor resolution is fairly standard, screen size is not. We recommend designing Web pages at a width of 580-pixels to fit comfortably within a 14-inch monitor and scanning images to fit within the page. Initial scanning for the Web may be 150 pixels per inch to give some leeway in resizing. Converting the working files to 72 pixels per inch gives a good approximation in a Web authoring program of an image's appearance on the Internet.

AN OVERVIEW OF FILE FORMATS

At the moment, the Internet supports three kinds of image formats: JPEG (Joint Photographic Experts Group), GIF (Graphic Interchange Format), and PNG (Portable Network Graphics). The JPEG format is often best for photographs or other continuous-tone images and GIF format is best for solid tone graphics and line art. (If you want to silhouette your photo or have parts of it be transparent it must be a GIF.) GIFs can be still images or a series of animated images. PNG files have better compression than GIFs but do not support animation.

COMPRESSION

Compression reduces the file size and consequently the loading time of images. GIF files achieve compression by reducing the number of colors in the

QUICK TIPS

Once your images and page files are finished, don't change their names or the hierarchy of your files and folders. Renaming a file or moving one to a different folder can break the link structure of your site.

It's wise to check the on-line appearance of your web pages by viewing them through different browsers, such as Nescape or Explorer, and making adjustments in your Web-authoring program.

Using Web-safe colors

HTML uses a palette limited to 216 colors. While it is possible to use up to 16 million colors on a Web page there is no guarantee that any colors except these 216 will display correctly on all systems. In Photoshop one may select colors from a swatch palette (**A**) or from a color picker (**B**) that displays a continuous spectrum divided into areas that correspond to Web-safe colors when the Only Web Colors box is checked.

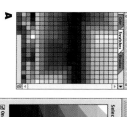

A

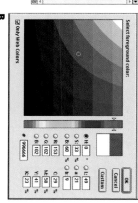

B

image while JPEG files use algorithms to denote changes in adjacent areas of color.

Once an image is compressed it cannot be uncompressed, edited and recompressed, so always save your source file under a different name.

COLOR RESTRICTIONS

A Web page is accessible to any Internet user, anywhere on the planet, via many types of equipment and browser software. Thus the appearance of a Web page will vary from viewer to viewer. Differences in the gamma curves used by monitors make the same colors look lighter on a Macintosh, for example, than on a Windows-based machine. To make Internet image color more consistent, a restricted palette of 216 colors was developed, known as *Web-safe* colors. Although advances in technology may soon render this a moot issue, it's a good idea to limit the graphic elements in your Web site, and any GIF files, to this palette. The colors in JPEG files, however, cannot be reduced to the Web-safe palette.

LEGIBILITY AND BACKGROUNDS

When using scans as backgrounds, be sure to keep text legibility in mind. Common sense dictates that background colors and images should be either dark or light in tone and low in contrast and that the color of any type placed over a background should contrast with the background color.

ADAPTING PRINTED PAGES TO THE WEB

Many publishers are creating Web versions of their magazines and newsletters. Conventional page layout files can be converted to HTML, though not without some sacrifices. In adapting a print publication for the Web one must yield control over many elements of the design. For example, the text fonts you specify can be overridden by the browser of the viewer and the restrictions of the 216 "Web-safe" colors make an exact match of PMS ink colors impossible. Type and layout formatting are retained when a PageMaker or Quark file is converted to PDF format, but PDF files are essentially graphic images and lack interactivity.

Re-purposing scans

(1) Although the photos in the newsletter were printed in black from grayscale images, they were initially scanned in color so that they might also be published on-line as a color JPEG or GIF files. The captions under the photos were typeset and included as part of the image file.

Adapting design elements

(2) The color block running down the left side of the newsletter page became a vertical background tile containing the site's navigation tools.

Headlines as graphics

(3) To preserve some of the fonts of the typeset newsletter the main headlines can be included as graphics files.

Variable text

(4) The width of any text blocks that are not anchored within tables will vary according to the user's browser window.

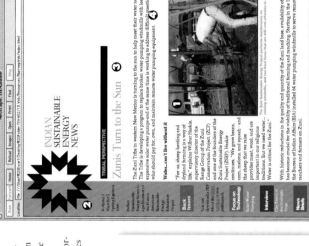

INDIAN SUSTAINABLE ENERGY NEWS

Volume 1, Number 2
Spring Equinox 1999

Indian Sustainable Energy News is a publication of the Native American Renewable Energy Education Project

TRIBAL PERSPECTIVE

Zunis Turn to the Sun

The Zuni Sustainable Energy Project performs maintenance on existing wind mills, and has fixed those that are still cost-effective to repair.

The Zuni Tribe in western New Mexico is turning to the sun to help meet their water needs. The Tribe is developing a program to replace broken water pumping windmills with less expensive solar water pumps—and at the same time is working to address difficult questions of who should pay for, own, and maintain remote water pumping equipment.

Water...can't live without it

"For us, sheep herding and dryland farming is a way of life," explains Wilbur Haskie, supervisory director of the Range Group of the Zuni Conservation Project (ZCP) and one of the founders of the Zuni Sustainable Energy Project (ZSEP). Haskie continues, "We grow beans, corn, melons, and squash - and the sheep that we raise provides meat, wool, and are important in our religious traditions. But we need water... Water is critical for the Zuni."

With historic reductions in the quality and quantity of water has become crucial for the viability of traditional farming and ranching. Starting in the 1930s, the Bureau of Indian Affairs (BIA) installed 64 water pumping windmills to serve remote ranchers and farmers on Zuni.

In the late 1970s, maintenance and repair of these windmills became too expensive for the BIA, and responsibility and ownership of the windmills was turned

Continued

DARREN SANCHEZ

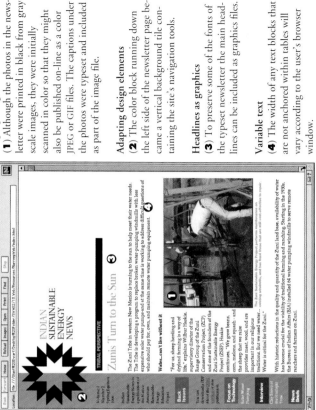

Netscape: ISENhome

INDIAN SUSTAINABLE ENERGY NEWS

Volume 1
Number 2
Spring Equinox
1999

Back Issues

You can download a PDF version of this publication

Focus on Technology — Solar Water Pumping

Interview

News Briefs

TRIBAL PERSPECTIVE

Zunis Turn to the Sun

The Zuni Tribe in western New Mexico is turning to the sun to help meet their water needs. The Tribe is developing a program to replace broken water-pumping windmills with less expensive solar water pumps-and at the same time is working to address difficult questions of who should pay for, own, and maintain remote water pumping equipment.

Water...can't live without it

"For us, sheep herding and dryland farming is a way of life," explains Wilbur Haskie, supervisory director of the Range Group of the Zuni Conservation Project (ZCP) and one of the founders of the Zuni Sustainable Energy Project (ZSEP). Haskie continues, "We grow beans, corn, melons, and squash - and the sheep that we raise provides meat, wool, and are important in our religious traditions. But we need water. Water is critical for the Zuni."

With historic reductions in the quality and quantity of the Zuni land base, availability of water has become crucial for the viability of traditional farming and ranching. Starting in the 1930s, the Bureau of Indian Affairs (BIA) installed 64 water pumping windmills to serve remote ranchers and farmers on Zuni.

The Zuni Sustainable Energy Project performs maintenance on existing windmills, and has fixed those that are still cost-effective to repair.

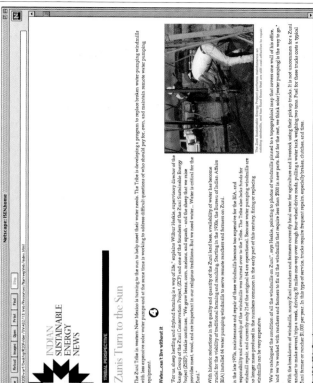
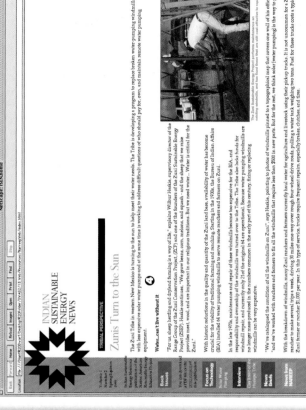

Netscape: ISENhome

INDIAN SUSTAINABLE ENERGY NEWS

Volume 1
Number 2
Spring Equinox
1999

Indian Sustainable Energy News is a publication of the Native American Renewable Energy Education Project

Back Issues

You can download a PDF version of this publication

Focus on Technology — Solar Water Pumping

Interview

News Briefs

TRIBAL PERSPECTIVE

Zunis Turn to the Sun

The Zuni Tribe in western New Mexico is turning to the sun to help meet their water needs. The Tribe is developing a program to replace broken water-pumping windmills with less expensive solar water pumps-and at the same time is working to address difficult questions of who should pay for, own, and maintain remote water pumping equipment.

Water...can't live without it

"For us, sheep herding and dryland farming is a way of life," explains Wilbur Haskie, supervisory director of the Range Group of the Zuni Conservation Project (ZCP) and one of the founders of the Zuni Sustainable Energy Project (ZSEP). Haskie continues, "We grow beans, corn, melons, and squash - and the sheep that we raise provides meat, wool, and are important in our religious traditions. But we need water. Water is critical for the Zuni."

With historic reductions in the quality and quantity of the Zuni land base, availability of water become crucial for the viability of traditional farming and ranching. Starting in the 1930s, the Bureau of Indian Affairs (BIA) installed 64 water pumping windmills to serve remote ranchers and farmers on Zuni.

In the late 1970s, maintenance and repair of these windmills became too expensive for the Tribe. The Tribe also lacks funds for windmill repair, and currently only 21 of the original 64 are operational. Because water pumping windmills are no longer mass-produced in the numbers common in the early part of this century, fixing or replacing windmills can be very expensive.

"We've catalogued the condition of all the windmills on Zuni," says Haskie, pointing to photos of windmills pinned to a topographical map that covers one wall of his office, "and we've worked with ranchers and farmers to fix all the windmills that require less than $500 in new parts. But for the rest, we think solar water pumping is the way to go."

With the breakdown of windmills, many Zuni ranchers and farmers currently haul water for agriculture and livestock using their pickup trucks. It is not uncommon for a Zuni rancher to make several trips a week, driving 30 miles one-way over rough four-wheel-drive roads, pulling a water tank weighing two tons. Fuel for these trucks require frequent repairs, especially brakes, clutches, and tires.

The Zuni Sustainable Energy Project performs maintenance on existing windmills, and has fixed those that are still cost-effective to repair.

Using Scans On-line

OPTIMIZING SCANNED IMAGES FOR THE WEB

Yes, you can take a great picture, scan it, and publish it on the World Wide Web. But will viewers find it worth the wait? Optimizing images for the Web is the art of compromise between image quality and loading time.

SIZE MATTERS

Nothing compares with the sheer drama of a large image, but concern about loading time means that images should be as small as possible, often leading to a Web page that looks like a sheet of postage stamps. (One way to get around the problem is to present the viewer with a smaller scale preview of the image which, when clicked, will link to a full-size version.)

As a rule, keep your images to a maximum width of 500 pixels and use slices to break down larger pictures into manageable chunks (See "Using Slices" on the facing page). Web authoring programs allow images to be re-sized by dragging a corner handle, but this can cause transmission delays and degradation in image quality. It's better to use an image editor to scale images.

Once you've arrived at an appropriate size for an image, the next step is to

QUICK TIP

When using Photoshop or ImageReady to prepare images for the Web it's often difficult to judge the best size, even when working in actual pixels scale at 72 pixels per inch. We've found that when images are viewed along with all the other images on the page, and amid the clutter of the browser's interface, they often look about 10% larger than you'd like. So trying making your images a little smaller than you think they should be.

determine the best file format and compression factor to make it hum over the wires.

CONSIDERING THE ALTERNATIVES

Image editing programs provide many possible choices in saving images for the Web.

GIF FORMAT

The most suitable format for lettering and non-photographic images (such as a logo or a border) is a GIF in *Indexed Color* format. Indexed color analyzes the colors that actually occur in an image, discards the unused parts of the color spectrum and reassigns pixels to the remaining colors in a custom palette.

Many images contain far fewer than 256 discernible colors. A portrait, for example, may consist primarily of flesh tones. Consequently, a tolerable image may be produced from as few as 32 colors.

GIFs may have *dithering* applied to them. Dithering is a method of producing intermediate colors by mixing two colors in a pattern of pixels. Dithering may reduce "banding" or unwanted posterization in images that have subtle tonal gradations.

JPEG FORMAT

The JPEG format, most suitable for pho-

Optimizing a scanned photo for the Web We recommend the JPEG format for most scanned photos that are to be published on the Internet. Adobe ImageReady provides a handy comparison of compression and format options so that you can see and select the best option. Note that as the file size and loading time decreases, the degree of image degradation increases.

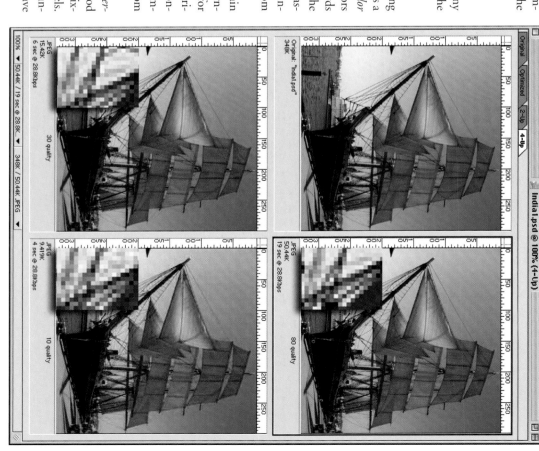

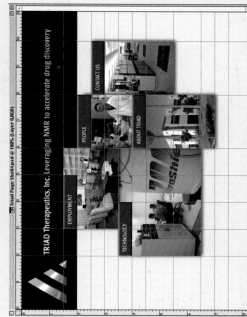

tographs, retains the whole color spectrum but discards image information where differences between adjacent color areas are less noticeable. As more and more compression is applied the colors remain accurate, but details of the image become increasingly distorted. Extreme compression results in the appearance of blocky shapes in large areas of color, such as skies, and noticeable fringing around the edges of objects, resembling the overuse of a sharpening filter (see page 23). Because a JPEG does not support transparency it cannot be used for silhouetted photos.

PNG FORMAT

The recently introduced PNG (Portable Network Graphics) format combines some of the advantages of GIF and JPEG, but may not yet be supported by all current versions of web browsers and web authoring programs.

As a general rule one should avoid using file formats that force users to update their browsers or acquire a special plug-in.

To make choosing the right format relatively painless we recommend using Adobe's ImageReady, or versions of Photoshop that incorporate ImageReady. Various format options may be viewed side-by-side with their respective file sizes and estimated loading times. The effects of restricted color palettes and degrees of compression can be compared before making a decision about final file format.

Saving graphic scans as GIFS
If your scan is a logo, lettering or a graphic with flat colors, save it for the Web as a GIF. The JPEG format produces unwanted compression artifacts in images of this kind, although it gives superior results for photographs.

Using noise to avoid banding
If your graphic contains subtle gradations, such as drop shadows (**C**), undesirable banding may occur (**D**). You can avoid the problem by applying noise and dithering when saving the image as a GIF (**E**).

GIF

JPEG

USING SLICES

Designing Web pages can sometimes be frustrating because of the limitations of the HTML environment. Using tables can help to make a page more organized and graphically pleasing, but sometimes tables don't appear in the Web browser the way they look in your HTML authoring program.

One way to gain control over the precise position of design elements is to use *slices*, a group of images that form a complete design, fitting neatly into an invisible table like a painting by Mondrian. Slices make it possible to design a Web page holistically, as a single entry with headlines, buttons, photos and graphics, and then cut it into smaller pieces that load more efficiently.

In this example two programs work in tandem to create a sliced Web page.

First we created a web page design in Photoshop, using layers to arrange scanned photos, type and other elements (**A**). Next we added guides to define the boundaries between the design elements.

Then we opened the Photoshop file in ImageReady and instructed the program to make slices as defined by the guides (**B**). (Several slices can be combined together to reduce their number).

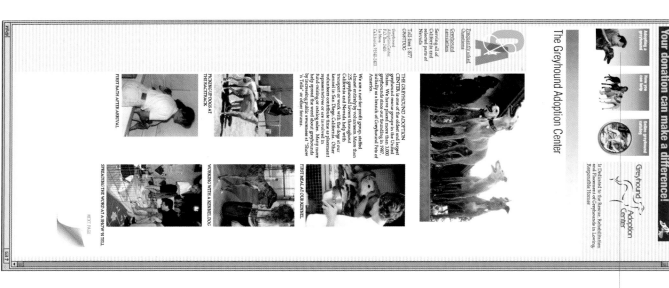

DEVELOPING AN ORGANIZATIONAL WEB SITE

Nonprofit organizations work to further a cause, meet certain societal needs and raise funds to continue their operation. The Internet has become an essential tool for such organizations to disseminate information and recruit new members. This Web site for the Greyhound Adoption Society uses photos of the dogs to plead their case. We wanted a site structure that could make the most of the huge library of available snapshots of dogs, owners and volunteers. Many of the photos provided by the Society had an iconic quality that made them suitable for use as navigational buttons.

Greyhounds are sleek and built for speed, but as pets they could not be shown outdoors without a leash. So gray striped backgrounds and grey fade bars were used to evoke swiftness. Some of the photos were silhouetted and saved as GIF files so that the shape of the image could stand out against the background.

The basic structure of the pages is a five-column table in which adjacent columns are sometimes combined to form a wider column for text and images.

Using scans as buttons
The navigation buttons on this Web site are scanned images that have been silhouetted, combined with type, and saved as GIF files. A larger version of the button photo appears at the head of each page, providing a visual link.

MAKING A FAMILY WEB SITE

In addition to business, news, commerce and non-profits, the Internet is awash with personal information. Autobiographies, self-promotion and family histories abound. In the hypothetical example shown here we used photos of one person, selected by a "hot spot" (see below) to weave a story through time. Large type dates were used as backgrounds. The headline, photo and text on each page were contained within a three-row, one column table in which all elements were centered. Cell padding created some distance between photos and text.

Using hot spots

Rather than using a separate button for navigation, it's possible to designate a specific area of an image to serve as a link to another page. The presence of the link is revealed when the cursor passes over the defined "hot spot" and turns into a pointing finger. Web authoring programs such as PageMill provide tools for drawing polygons to create invisible buttons on any part of an image. A group family photo, for example might contain as many hot-spots as there are people, linking each to their personal histories.

MAKING WEB ANIMATIONS WITH SCANS

Creators of Web sites that include moving pictures often seem to think that they are making an interactive DVD or CD-ROM. This is a mistake because the current state of Internet technology is too clumsy to support continuous motion and interactivity at the same time. What starts as a creative inspiration can become a source of annoyance for the viewer. Thus, we advise caution in incorporating animation into Web page design.

Rollovers and animated GIFs are supported by most browsers. However, animation formats that require the user to download special plugs-ins, player programs and the like should be avoided.

Using Rollovers
Rollovers, like hot spots, are a more subtle way of defining an interactive element than creating a stand-alone button. When the cursor passes over a rollover object, the object graphic changes. This requires the creation of two different graphics for each rollover button. You can modify a scan by adding a glow effect, for example, to use as the rollover state.

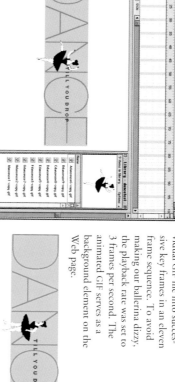

Using Animated GIFs
In this example we made a series of line art scans of a dancer in various poses (from *2001 Decorative Cuts and Ornaments*, Dover 1988) and compiled them into an animated GIF file using Macromedia Flash. This was accomplished by inserting each scan as an individual GIF file into successive key frames in an eleven frame sequence. To avoid making our ballerina dizzy, the playback rate was set to 3 frames per second. The animated GIF serves as a background element on the Web page.

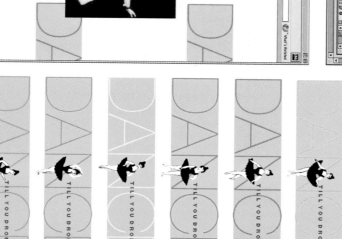

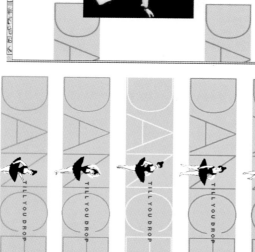

Resources

PRINTED CLIP ART

Art Direction Book Company
10 East 39th Street
New York, NY 10016
212/889-6500

Crown Publishers
Crown Publishing Group
Random House
1540 Broadway
New York, NY 10036
212/782-9000
www.randomhouse.com

Dover Publications
31 East 2nd Street
Mineola, NY 11501
(no phone or web site; write to request Pictorial Archives catalog)

Rockport Publishers
33 Commercial Street
Gloucester, MA 01930
978/282-9590
www.rockpub.com

Stemmer House Publishers
2627 Caves Road
Owings Mills, MD 21117-2998
410/363-3690
www.stemmer.com

ROYALTY-FREE IMAGES

Artbeats Software, Inc.
P.O. Box 709
Myrtle Creek, OR 97457
800/444-9392, 503/863-4429
503/863-4547 fax
www.artbeats.com

Classic PIO Partners
87 East Green Street, Suite 809
Pasadena, CA 91105
626/564-8106
www.classicpartners.com

Dynamic Graphics
6000 N. Forest Park Drive
Peoria, IL 61614
800/255-8800
www.dgusa.com

EyeWire
8 South Idaho Street
Seattle, WA 98134
800/661-9410
www.eyewire.com

PhotoDisc, Inc.
701 North 34th Street, Suite 400
Seattle, WA 98103
800/528-3472
www.photodisc.com

SOFTWARE

Adobe Systems, Inc.
345 Park Avenue
San Jose, CA 95110
408/536-6000
www.adobe.com
Maker of:
GoLive
Illustrator
InDesign
PageMaker
PageMill
Photoshop
Premiere
Streamline

Corel Corporation
1600 Carling Avenue
Ottawa, Ontario K1Z 8R7
Canada
613/728-8200
www.corel.com
Maker of:
CorelDRAW
Corel Painter
CorelPHOTO-PAINT

Macromedia, Inc.
600 Townsend Street
San Francisco, CA 94103
415/252-2000
www.macromedia.com
Maker of:
Dreamweaver
Fontographer
Flash
FreeHand

Quark, Inc.
1800 Grant Street
Denver, CO 80203
303/894-8888
www.quark.com
Maker of: QuarkXPress

BOOKS

Real World Scanning and Halftones, 2nd. Edition
by David Blatner, Glenn Fleishman
and Steve Roth
from Peachpit Press, 1998
2414 Sixth Street
Berkeley, CA 94710
800/283-9444
www.peachpit.com

DESKTOP SCANNERS

Epson
3840 Kilroy Airport Way
Long Beach, CA 90806
800/873-7766
www.epson.com

Hewlett Packard
3000 Hanover Street
Palo Alto, CA 94304
650/857-5518
www.hewlettpackard.com

Microtek
800/654-4160
www.microtek.com

UMAX Technologies
3561 Gateway Blvd.
Freemont, CA 94538
510/651-4000
www.umax.com

Index

About the Authors

JANET ASHFORD is a freelance writer, graphic designer and musician and the coauthor of five books on computer graphics: *Getting Started with 3D: A Designer's Guide to 3D Graphics and Illustration* (Peachpit Press, 1998), *Start with a Scan: A Guide to Transforming Scanned Photos and Objects into High Quality Art* (Peachpit Press, 1996, first edition), *Adobe Illustrator: A Visual Guide for the Mac* (Graphic-Sha/Addison-Wesley, 1995), *Aldus PageMaker: A Visual Guide for the Mac* (Graphic-Sha/Addison-Wesley, 1994), and *The Verbum Book of PostScript Illustration* (M&T Books, 1990).

Since 1989 Janet has written "how-to" articles on computer graphics for computer and design magazines including *Macworld*, *MacUser*, *Step-By-Step Electronic Design*, *Step-By-Step Graphics*, *Dynamic Graphics* and *Print*. She has created designs for books, newsletters and brochures and produced original illustrations for posters, textbooks, and magazines. She currently teaches classes in digital art and design at the Mendocino Art Center in Mendocino, California.

Janet has worked as a fine artist for the past 30 years, creating drawings, paintings and posters with watercolor, pen-and-ink, oils, acrylics, and silk screen. She is also a musician and composed and performed the original music for the interactive Photo CD that accompanies *The Official Photo CD Handbook* (Peachpit Press, 1995). She performs regularly on violin with various folk music groups in Mendocino—including The Northern Troupe, Last Night's Fun and The Fort Bragg Philharmonic—and has composed a number of original jigs, reels and waltzes.

Before becoming involved with computer graphics, Janet wrote many books and articles on childbirth including *The Whole Birth Catalog* (Crossing Press, 1983) and *Birth Stories: The Experience Remembered* (Crossing Press, 1984) and for 9 years published *Childbirth Alternatives Quarterly*. Her video *The Timeless Way: A History of Birth from Ancient to Modern Times* (InJoy Videos, 1998) was a winner of the 1999 National Educational Media Network Gold Apple Award.

Janet has a B.A. in psychology from the University of California at Los Angeles. She and her three children live in Mendocino, California, on the coast about 120 miles north of San Francisco. Ashford's web site is www.jashford.com.

JOHN ODAM is an award-winning graphic designer and the principal of Beardsley and Company, Inc. John grew up in England and graduated from Leicester College of Art. He has worked in publishing since 1967 as both a designer and art director. John was for many years art director of the early desktop-published *Verbum* magazine and has contributed articles to *Step-By-Step*, *Bright Ideas* and *Before & After*. He is also the author of *Start with a Digital Camera* (Peachpit Press, 1999), a book on the creative uses of digital photography. He has contributed many articles and illustrations to magazines and books throughout the world.

John is also a keen musician, playing traditional Celtic and American music on mandolin, fiddle and mandocello. You can visit John's Website and purchase a unique product at www.beardshampoo.com.

Janet Ashford and John Odam are also the authors of *Getting Started with 3D: A Designer's Guide to 3D Graphics and Illustration*.